W9-CJR-364

The Illustrated Encyclopedia of the *Animal Kingdom*

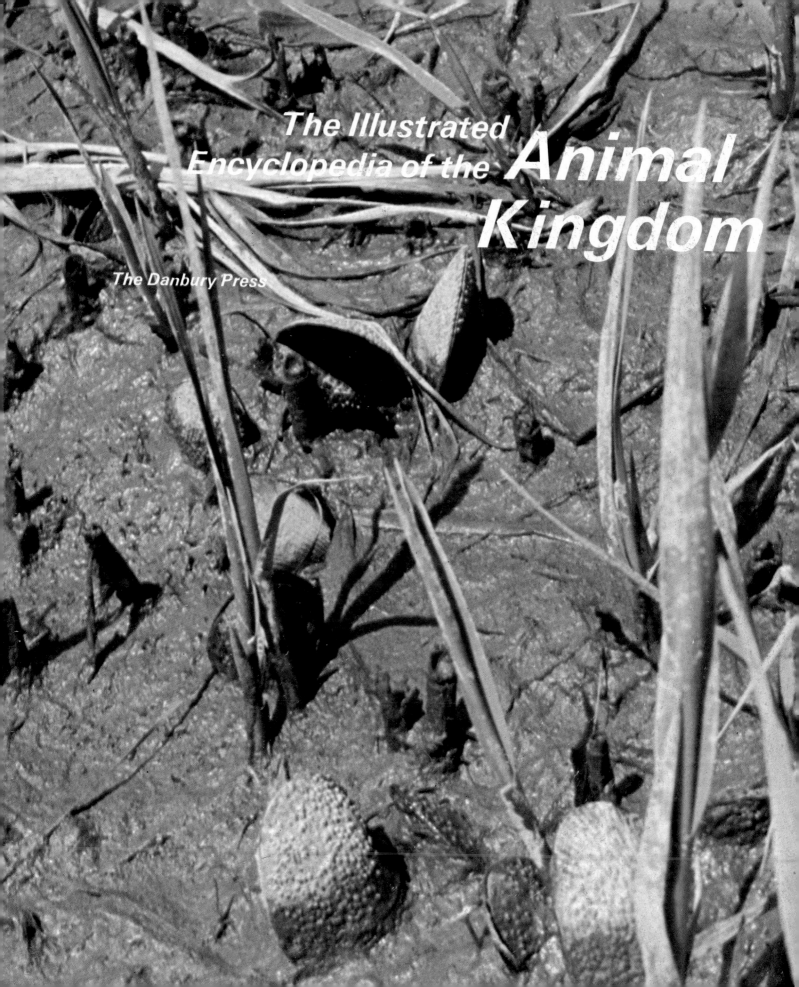

The Illustrated
Encyclopedia of the Animal
Kingdom

The Danbury Press

Editorial: Herbert Kondo—Editor
Jenny E. Tesar—Senior Editor
Deena Cloud—Associate Editor
Wesley F. Strombeck—Associate Editor
Lynn T. Kagan—Assistant Editor
Constance Hintz—Editorial Assistant
Kathleen Leerburger—Indexer

Art and Design: Jack Jaget

Production Supervision: The Stonehouse Press

Editorial, original English edition: Percy Knauth, Dale McAdoo, James Cox

Zoological Consultant: William E. Old, Jr., Scientific Assistant, Department of Living Invertebrates, The American Museum of Natural History, New York, New York

The Danbury Press, a division of Grolier Enterprises, Inc.
Publisher—Robert B. Clarke.

ISBN 0-7172-8100-0
Library of Congress Catalog Card Number 71-141898
© 1968 by Fratelli Fabbri Editori, Milan
Text: © 1972 Grolier Enterprises, Inc.
Illustrations*: © 1968, 1971, 1972 Fratelli Fabbri Editori, Milan

*Except those illustrations set forth below in Photo Credits
as not being owned by Fratelli Fabbri Editori.

PHOTO CREDITS

F. Bin—25, 48, 49, 50, 68; Bucciarelli—14, 23, 28, 31, 52, 61, 65, 66, 83, 87, 89, 91, 104, 114, 128; Cauvin—140; C. P. Clausen—46; Bruce Coleman Ltd.—J. Burton—137; W. Harstrick—123; R. K. Murton—73; Prof. Conci—140; Prof. Carlo Consiglio—96, 107; Domenichini—46; Forni—56; F. Frill—33, 56, 64; Fulton—45; L. Gaggero—24, 63; G. S. Giacomelli—14, 15, 20, 21, 26, 27, 42, 51, 63, 69, 84, 100, 120, 122, 124, 126; Giussani—11, 33, 41, 55, 72, 77, 80, 81, 84, 87, 89, 91, 98, 99, 106, 118, 120, 127, 129, 130, 132, 135, 136, 142; G. M. Grislowod—46; Groppi—25, 32, 68, 69; G. E. Hyde—10, 19, 29, 96, 124; Lombardi—15, 41, 75, 93, 108, 128; Marro-Express—22, 53, 101, 118, 138, 141; G. Mazza—76; N.H.P.A.-E. Elma—7; W. Zeph—9, 12, 16; National Historical Photographs—113, 137; Paul Popper—8, 38, 39, 40, 59, 62, 91, 110, 111, 138; Prenzel—13; C. Ravizza—32, 42, 77, 78, 115; E. Robba—18, 55; Roebild-Siebert—95; G. Russo—43; Dr. Sella—14, 15; Silvestri—70; Sturani—47; U.S.I.S.—94; G. Varlati—88, 90; V-Dia—54; W. M. Wheeler—42; C. Zeiss—34, 38; Z.F.A.—6; Zinna—46.

*Robert S. DeSanto—2, 3, 26, 27, 30, 31, 46, 47, 72, 73.

Printed in the United States of America

567899876543

CONTENTS

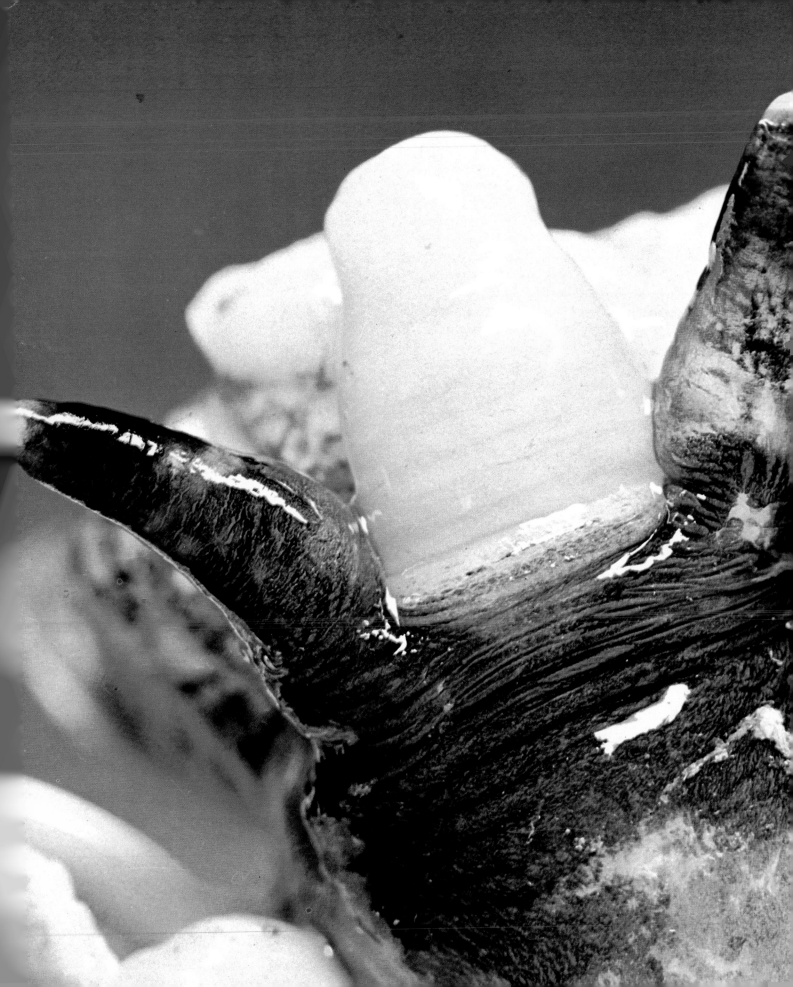

The Mollusks

Few of us who walk along beaches can resist picking up and admiring a shell. If it is a large clam shell we may take it home, to use as a baking dish. If we find lots of tiny shells with holes in them we may string them, to wear as a necklace. Or we may be collectors, identifying and saving every type of shell we find.

One doesn't have to be on a beach to find shells, or animals with shells. Snails, for example, are easily found in country gardens and city parks. Even on some of the highest mountains of the world there are shells to be found—fossil shells of animals that lived millions of years ago, when the earth that formed these mountains was deep beneath the ocean.

Animals such as clams and snails are mollusks, members of the invertebrate phylum Mollusca. Like all the other animal phyla, the members of the Mollusca exhibit great variety. Here we find not only clams and snails, oysters and mussels, but also octopuses and squids.

At first glance, the clam and the octopus don't look at all alike. Closer examination, however, reveals that they share many features, features that are common to all mollusks. All mollusks are bilaterally symmetrical and unsegmented. The majority have a shell; those that are without shells as adults have formed and lost one during their embryonic period. Finally, all mollusks have a *foot*. The foot is used by the snail for creeping, by a clam for digging, and by the squid for catching food. In some groups the foot is used to attach the mollusk to the substratum.

Although mollusks are most numerous in the sea, they also live in fresh water, brackish water, and on land. Mollusks have been found almost everywhere—from the deepest waters to the highest mountains, in the Arctic and in the tropics. They range in size from barely visible sea snails to the 85-foot-long giant squid.

Altogether there are some 100,000 species of mollusks. They are grouped into seven classes, according to the characteristics of their foot, gills, mantle, nervous system, and shell.

The class Monoplacophora includes one genus of primitive mollusks that until recently had been thought to be extinct. The Aplacophora are wormlike mollusks without shells. The Polyplacophora include the chitons. The Pelecypoda are the bivalves, mollusks such as clams, scallops, and oysters. The Scaphopoda are the tusk shells. The Gastropoda include the snails. And the class Cephalopoda contains the squids, cuttlefish, and octopuses.

More than 30,000 fossil species of mollusks are known. Mollusk shells have been found among fossils of the Lower Cambrian strata laid down at least 600 million years ago. However, mollusks may have existed much earlier as naked, soft-bodied forms that left no known fossil evidence.

In Precambrian eras, before erosion from the continents saturated the seas with mineral salts, the formation of shells may have been impossible. In later eras, calcium from

The strange-looking object on the opposite page is the head of a sea snail. We can see quite plainly the two tentacles. Between them is a proboscis, which is used to ingest food.

The respiratory pore of this land snail, Cepaea nemoralis, *is clearly visible beneath the edge of its shell.*

the sea water had to be extracted by marine animals; in some, this metabolic waste product became a hard growth and, finally, a protective covering.

Not all mollusks left good fossil records. It is easy to find the remains of one of the tusk shells in a rock of the Cenozoic era or the twisted cone of a prehistoric marine snail in layers of Mesozoic origin. However, creatures such as the nudibranchs and aplacophorans had no shell and rarely left a fossil record.

Other classes have left a fascinating history. From fossils, it is known that there were once more than 10,000 species of cephalopods and that they had shells. Today, the nautiloids are represented by a mere five species of pearly *Nautilus*, but there are more than 3,000 fossil species of this group.

An offshoot of the primitive nautiloid stock was the ammonite, so-called because its coiled shell resembled the ram's-head emblem of ancient Egypt's god, Ammon. Other peoples who found these common fossils thought they were the petrified remains of coiled snakes, and called them serpent stones. The largest ammonites had shells up to 9 feet across.

Shells

The first thing you notice when you pick up most mollusks is their shell. The mollusks are classified partly on the characteristic form of their shells. In the Scaphopoda, the shell is a single, hollow tube that is long, conical, and curved like an elephant's tusk. In the bivalves, as the name suggests, the shell is formed of two valves that are joined by a ligament. The chiton shell has eight dove-tailed plates attached to a leathery ligament. Gastropod shells usually form a spiral. Among the cephalopods, only a few species, notably the nautiluses, have an external shell; in the others the shell either does not exist or survives only as an internal plate called the *pen*.

In all mollusks except gastropods there are pairs of symmetrically arranged muscles that attach the shell to the body. In the gastropods there is a single muscle joining the body to the inside of the spiral shell.

The shapes of mollusk shells, particularly among the gastropods, have an infinite variety. In gastropods, the shell most often coils in a spiral, forming whorls that gradually increase in size. In most cases the shell

The shell of an adult snail protects the animal against its enemies. However, the shells of these young snails (right) do little to protect them. As the translucent shine suggests, these shells are very fragile.

8

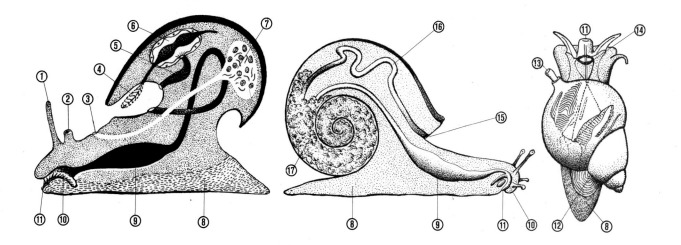

spirals to the right—we say it is right-handed.

A system of irregular spirals leads to the formation of globular shells, while whorls developing on a single plane form disclike shells. Often the final whorl, which may be globular, conical, cylindrical, or oval, shows a marked reduction of the spiral. If the spiral is clearly evident, with numerous crevices, the shell is turreted; and if, at the same time, the base of the shell is extended in a canal, the result is a fusiform, or funnel-shaped, shell.

Ornamentation. In addition to form, shells are also distinguished by ornamentation, which depends on the secretory activity of the mantle. If secretion is regular and uniform, the shell has a smooth surface; if the secretion is irregular, the surface will be ornate.

The shells of bivalves are generally less complex than those of the gastropods in form and relief. But they are not by any means all alike. In some bivalves both valves are roughly equal, in others they are not. Equilateral shells occur when the *umbos* (the protuberances on each valve above the hinge) are central. The shell is called inequivalve when the umbos are not on the

median line. Bivalves also have their own characteristic ornamentation, including ridges, spines, and other outgrowths.

Growth lines constitute one form of ornamentation in almost all shells. Development of the shell is not continuous; periodically, growth stops. When the animal resumes its secretions, fine lines are formed. These lines, concentric in bivalves and parallel to the lip in gastropods, are useful in determining the approximate age of the mollusk.

Many mollusks have special *chromogenic glands* located on the margin of the mantle. These glands secrete colored pigments that stain the calcium carbonate of the ordinarily white shell. If the glands are in continuous series and if they are steadily active, the shell will be a solid color. If they secrete continuously but are some distance from each other, spiral lines will appear. If the glands work intermittently, the color will show as dotted lines. In some cases, groups of adjacent glands secrete different pigments, creating multicolored designs of infinite variety. Coloration is amazingly identical in some species, while in others it varies from one individual to another.

Shell Formation. Probably the most remarkable thing about mollusks is the way they

These diagrams illustrate the major anatomical features of snails. A and B depict marine snails; C is a freshwater or land snail. The following parts are labeled:
1. *tentacle*
2. *eye*
3. *genital pore*
4. *gills*
5. *nephridium*
6. *heart cavity*
7. *reproductive organs*
8. *foot*
9. *stomach*
10. *radula*
11. *mouth*
12. *operculum*
13. *statocyst*
14. *periesophageal ring*
15. *anus*
16. *intestine*
17. *hepatopancreas*

build shells from lime extracted from sea water. The only tool they use for this construction is the *mantle,* a thin, fleshy fold of tissue that surrounds the organs of the animal's body. Examination under a microscope shows that the mantle is provided with a network of minute tubes, each of which excretes tiny particles of lime. These specks, almost invisible, form a thin layer that cements to a base of *conchyolin,* a hornlike substance produced by the animal. As additional layers are added, the shell grows in thickness.

Usually a shell is composed of three layers. The outside is a rough, horny skin of organic matter or a porcelainlike layer of vertical calcite crystals. Beneath this is a second calcite or aragonite layer with the crystals arranged in a different direction. On the inside is a third layer, which is composed of porcelainlike material. Shells with pearly linings called *nacre* are generally found in the more primitive species. This iridescent, or pearly, effect is caused by the arrangement of the minute crystals and the play of light on them.

The growth of the shell is linked to various factors, such as a suitable temperature and a rich food supply. In a normal environment, for example, the common limpet may take 16 years to reach a diameter of 1 inch. In an environment rich in organic material the limpet will double its size in only three years. It must pay for its rich existence, however, with a considerably shorter lifespan than slower-growing limpets.

The jaws of snails show considerable variety (below right). But because such variations exist within an individual species, jaw structure is not a perfect guide for species identification.

Anatomy

Most mollusks have a shell, head, foot, mantle, and visceral mass. However, not all of these structures are present in all mollusks. The head is equipped with mouth appendages in certain mollusks and with most of the special sense organs. The foot, on the ventral, or lower, side, varies in size and shape; however, it is always a fleshy, highly muscular, contractile projection.

Mantle. The mantle is a fold of tissue covering the visceral mass. Not only does the mantle secrete the shell, but the breathing apparatus—the gills or lungs—is formed from modified mantle tissue, as are the siphons, through which water enters and leaves the body. In some groups the mantle is also involved in food-getting. In others it is used in locomotion.

Jaws. A jaw is found in all mollusks except clams. It occupies the upper part of the mouth and is generally crescent shaped and vertically grooved. It may be formed by a single plate, or by a number of plates united by a membrane or fused to one another. This horny organ varies in form from one species to another, and thus is useful as a means of identification.

Radula. The radula is a structure peculiar to mollusks. It is present in all groups except the bivalves. Located in a sac at the back of the mouth, in its most common form

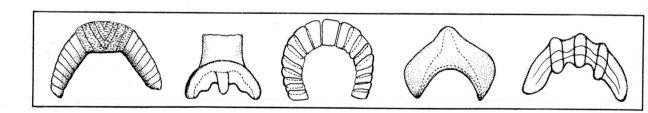

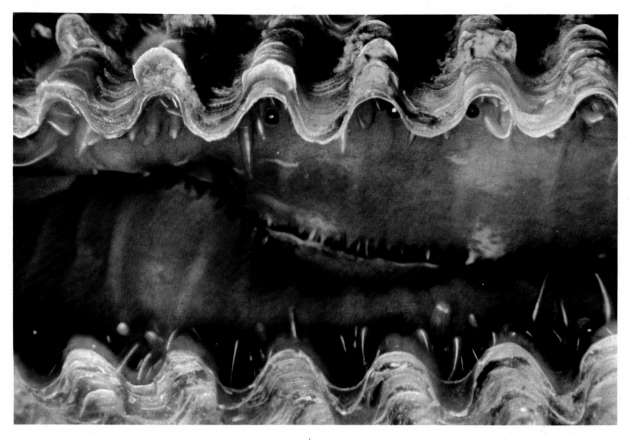

Pearllike eyes peer out along the mantle border of a scallop (left). These tiny eyes, which may be bright blue in color, make scallops, thorny oysters, and cockles unique among bivalves. Most other bivalves do not have true eyes. Rather, they have receptors that are sensitive to any changes in light intensity.

The diagram below shows the comparatively simple anatomy of a bivalve: (1) mouth; (2) stomach; (3) heart cavity; (4) foot.

it resembles a file. It may contain as many as 18,000 tiny, rasplike teeth arranged in transverse rows, sometimes in symmetrical series on either side of a central tooth. The size of the radula and the number, size, and pattern of the teeth on it vary greatly from one species to another.

The radula is a beltlike structure that works by moving back and forth over a cartilaginous tongue (the *odontophore*) like a rope in a pulley. The odontophore and radula can be extended from the mouth. The

radula scrapes the substratum, loosening food particles, which are then brought into the mouth. The extension and withdrawal of the radula are controlled by muscles attached to the odontophore.

The teeth of the radula wear down with use. New teeth grow continually at the back end of the structure. As the front teeth wear down, a new part of the belt moves forward.

Digestive System. The digestive system begins with the mouth, or buccal opening.

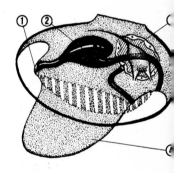

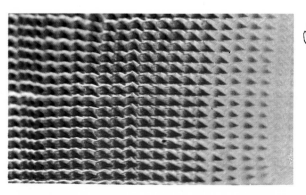

The filelike tongue, or radula, of a mollusk (far left) is covered with many rows of teeth. These teeth, shown in the detailed diagram (near left), may number as many as 18,000 in some species.

Mucus-secreting salivary glands open into this cavity. Food particles scraped and brought into the mouth by the radula become trapped in the mucus. From the mouth, the food passes down a short, tubular esophagus to the stomach.

Part of the stomach is lined with chitin and part with cilia. In the cilia-lined portion, which is used for sorting food particles, are the openings to a pair of digestive glands (or livers). In the stomach the food particles become separated from the mucus strands. The particles are sorted by size; the lighter ones pass to the digestive glands, while the over-sized ones are passed into the intestine, where they are formed into fecal pellets.

In such primitive forms as the chiton, the long intestine leading away from the stomach is more or less straight. In snails the intestine follows the turns of the spiral and twists forward so that the anus opens in the front of the body near the head. The digestive gland of the snail, called the hepatopancreas, takes up a good part of the shell.

The digestive system of bivalves is always simple. The mouth is an oval opening without maxilla, radula, or salivary glands. A very short esophagus terminates in a stomach into which the excretory canals of the liver, or hepatopancreas, open. The liver accounts for a large part of the visceral mass.

In the cephalopods, the throat leads to a long esophagus and a gizzard. The intestine is curved in the form of a U and connects with the outside through the funnel, a conical tube projecting beyond the collar on the underside of the head.

Some mollusks have very simple light receptors. Others, such as the octopus, have well-developed eyes (right). The octopus eye is similar to a human eye. Light passes through the pupil; a lens focuses the image on the retina.

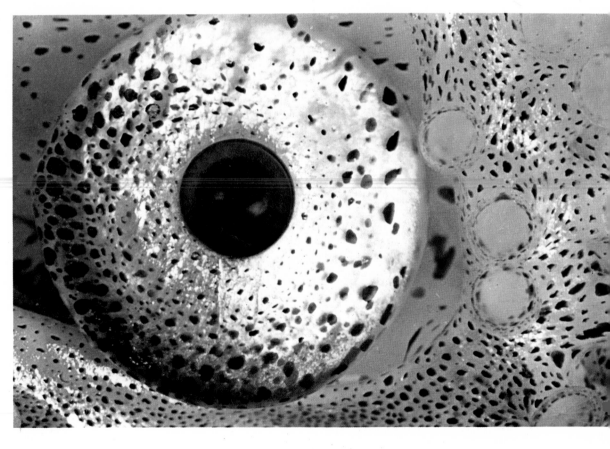

Circulatory System. The circulatory system of mollusks consists of a specialized pumping organ, the heart, some blood vessels, and a system of sinuses. It is an open circulatory system—that is, the blood is not completely confined to vessels.

Blood passes from the gills to two chambers in the heart called auricles. It then passes to a chamber called the ventricle. The contraction of the ventricle pumps the blood into the aorta, a large vessel that branches to form many smaller vessels. From these small vessels, the blood enters sinuses and bathes the body tissues directly. It then passes to the gills and empties back into the heart.

In most mollusks the blood is bluish; the color is due to the presence of a copper-containing respiratory pigment called *hemocyanin*. In a few mollusks the blood contains hemoglobin, and in these groups the blood is red.

Respiratory System. Some mollusks have a single pair of gills; others have two or more pairs. In the nudibranchs, respiratory organs known as cerata are arranged throughout the length of the body.

Freshwater and land snails breathe by means of a lung in the mantle cavity. The lung opens to the outside through pores located on either side of the body. The animal can close the pores at will—aquatic species to keep out water, and land dwellers to prevent evaporation. Freshwater snails, it should be noted, must surface from time to time to fill their mantle cavity with air.

Nervous System and Sensory Organs. The nervous system varies in complexity among the various groups. It is essentially formed of masses of nerve tissue called *ganglia*, which are interconnected. Its basic features are the cerebral ganglia, near the mouth, which supply the eyes and tentacles; the pedal ganglia, which serve the foot; and the pleural ganglia, serving the mantle, heart, and visceral organs—the latter by way of the visceral ganglia.

The sense organs include the tentacles, eyes, and statocysts. The statocysts are baglike organs containing grains of sand; they are involved with the sense of balance.

The sensory organs are highly developed for sight and touch. Gastropods and cephalopods have eyes on their heads. In some bivalves, there are eyes located on pipelike siphons and on the margins of the mantle; but in the many bivalves that have no eyes, the entire surface of the body is sensitive to light.

The eyes of cephalopods deserve special mention. The Canadian zoologist N. J. Berrill once said: "I think if you asked any zoologist to select the single most startling

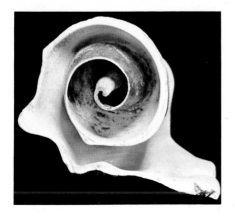

Each snail of the species Cepaea nemoralis *has both male and female sex organs. But a snail cannot fertilize its own eggs. Therefore, when two snails mate (left center), each fertilizes the eggs of its partner.*

The graceful spiral shell formed by a snail of the genus Strombus *is shown in transverse section (left).*

feature in the whole animal kingdom, the chances are he would say . . . not the human eye, which by any account is an organ amazing beyond belief, nor the squid-octopus eye, but the fact that these two eyes, man's and squid's, are alike in almost every detail."

Each, for example, has a transparent cornea. Both are described as "camera eyes," because like a camera, they admit light into a dark chamber through an opening (pupil) in a diaphragm (iris) behind which is a lens that focuses the light on a light-sensitive film (retina).

When two unrelated or very distantly related groups possess similar structures with similar functions and there is no possibility of a common ancestor, it must be presumed the structures evolved independently. This is called convergent evolution. The similarity between squid eyes and human eyes is one of its most remarkable examples.

A female Helix aspersa *(below) lays eggs. Like many mollusks, this snail will not protect the eggs. Thus she has taken great care in selecting a safe place for them to develop.*

Reproduction. In most mollusks the sexes are separate, although some are hermaphrodites and have both male and female sex organs. However, even among the hermaphroditic forms, reproduction is generally by cross-fertilization. In some groups fertilization is internal, while in others it is external.

The reproductive organs vary considerably with the different groups.

Marine gastropods, for the most part, have separate sexes and simple genital organs. Males have a fairly large testicle embedded in the liver and connected by a canal to the penis, which may be external and similar to a third tentacle, or may be inserted in the right tentacle. In females, the ovary is also embedded in the liver, and the long oviduct generally opens in the left part of the body, just below the head.

The genital organs of freshwater and land snails are far more complex. These creatures are generally hermaphrodites with a single genital orifice through which both male and female organs open. In some, the female organ is closely linked with the male organ. But individuals cannot fertilize themselves; fertilization only occurs, and occurs reciprocally, with the mating of two individuals.

In the viviparous freshwater species, the female has a copulatory sac in which the eggs are incubated until the young develop and emerge.

Some freshwater and terrestrial snails have a special organ called a *dart sac* that produces small, chalky shafts that the individuals shoot at each other before copulation. The function of this organ has not yet been defined, but it is generally assumed that the activity serves to excite the animals.

Bivalves are rarely true hermaphrodites. The symmetrical male or female glands may be seen only under the microscope. They do not have copulatory organs, and fertilization is almost always external.

Although wide variations exist, the general sex pattern among cephalopods is the

same for all but a few highly specialized species. There are separate sexes. One of the arms of the male is modified into a sex organ called a *hectocotyle*. This arm is used to plant the sperm on or inside the female's oviduct. In the argonauts and a few related octopuses, the thin end of the modified arm actually breaks away and remains in the female.

Inconsistency seems to be the hallmark of the sex life of mollusks. The majority of species, as we have learned, have separate sexes, although there are entire groups in which hermaphroditism predominates. But the distinction is not always clear. In some cases sex changes with age; in others, separate sexes and hermaphroditism coexist in the same species. Sexual dimorphism (differences in physical appearance between the two sexes) is not obvious, but there are a few exceptions. The female argonaut is at least ten times as large as the male, although in the gastropods the female is only slightly larger.

Fertilization usually takes place at the end of winter or the beginning of spring and is generally accomplished by copulation. Other methods of reproduction include such primitive forms as self-fertilization, external fertilization, and parthenogenesis (production of offspring by female cells without benefit of union with male cells). However, parthenogenesis is very rare among the mollusks.

Variety also exists in the manner of egg-laying, although most mollusks consistently take great care in selecting the place where the eggs will lie. Some deep-sea species rise almost to the surface to lay their eggs in a light, warm zone. Some land species, on the other hand, prepare a nest hole in the earth almost 2 feet deep. In this hole the temperature and humidity will be constant. Some rare species of gastropods hatch their eggs inside their bodies. Others place a certain number of eggs in a tough-skinned egg case, which is sometimes in the form of a ribbon that may be more than a yard long. The cases from a number of females may be stuck together in masses.

As a general rule, mollusks do not protect their newly laid eggs. Again there are exceptions, and in this regard the behavior of the female octopus is especially significant. Not only does she hide her eggs in empty bivalve shells or other submerged objects, but she also remains beside them for weeks, fanning them with water. In some cases the female mollusk will incubate her eggs within her mantle cavity, carefully placing them in the most secure position. In

The chiton Acanthopleura spiniger *(right) has an armorlike shell composed of eight plates. These plates overlap, rather like shingles. Among the most primitive of mollusks, chitons live on the sides and undersides of rocks. They feed on algae and other minute organisms.*

The wormlike mollusk Promecomenia sluiteri *(below) inhabits the Arctic Ocean. Like all aplocophorans, it does not have a shell. Aplocophorans and chitons belong to the class Polycophora.*

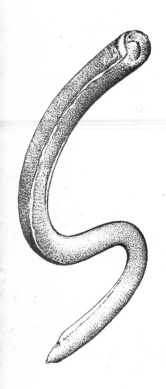

some highly evolved species of marine snails, the mother's body also serves as a refuge for the newborn, who return to it after brief excursions into the outside world.

Within a few hours after fertilization, a mollusk egg divides into numerous cells and forms a rudimentary digestive tube. In this stage of development the embryo is called a *gastrula*. In a short time, by continuing cell division and differentiation, the gastrula develops various organs and tissues. In its initial stages, the embryo is immobile. But by the time its outer surface has become ciliated, it has become a larva that is capable of swimming. Since many bivalves lead fixed lives, the ability of their larvae to swim is a valuable aid in dispersion.

Larval Stages. The larvae of more primitive mollusks, those reproducing by external fertilization, develop a number of ciliary bands. In some bivalves and in most of the snails, the larva has a single band of cilia in front of the mouth. The ciliary band is either absent or rudimentary in embryos that remain within the security of the egg case and have no need to swim, and it is nonexistent in the cephalopods.

In its earliest stages, the ciliated larva is called a *trochophore*. A short time later, when it forms a rudimentary foot and primitive shell, the larva is called a *veliger*. The shell of the veliger is horny and quite different from that of an adult. Even nudibranchs, which have no shell at maturity, develop one temporarily during the veliger stage.

The time lapse between fertilization of the eggs and development into the larval stage is sometimes amazingly short—less than 24 hours in the species with external fertilization. The period is a few days longer in those species with internal fertilization. In one unusual case embryonic development takes several months. Generally speaking, when the embryo is not protected, the phase passes rapidly. But when the embryo is secure in an egg case, where it can feed on the food reserve formed by the mass of unfertilized eggs that is always present, its development is slow and gradual.

Development is also affected by temperature. A species that takes 7 days to reach the larval stage in the Mediterranean, for example, will require about 15 days in the cooler northern seas.

The ciliary phase ends when the foot is transformed into a locomotor organ. At that time the aquatic mollusks fall to the sea bed to begin their normal adult lives. The shell begins to calcify, and it covers, continues, or replaces the larval shell.

Mobility is necessary at this stage if the larva is to complete its metamorphosis into an adult; it must find a suitable environment where it may continue to grow. If it fails in this search it will die.

Adulthood. As development continues, the shell begins to take on adult shape and color characteristics. The young shell is smoother and more fragile than the adult; the lip is sharp; the pigmentation less vivid; and in the appropriate groups, the turns of the spiral are fewer in number.

The duration of the youthful stage varies greatly with the species—it may be a few days or a few years. But in all cases its end is signalized by sexual maturity, which can be recognized by a swelling of the shell's external lip. This swelling, common to many species, sometimes marks the end of growth. Many mollusks, however, after a pause that is usually linked to a reproductive phase, resume their growth. In these cases, the swelling of the lip either remains as an axial cord or is reabsorbed.

It is curious to note that in most mollusks there is little relationship between size and age. Some sexually mature animals are half the size of young members of the same species. However, only in sexual maturity does the mollusk shell develop its richest coloring and ornamentation.

As old age creeps up on the mollusk, reproductive activity comes to a halt and pigmentation and ornamentation of the shell begin to diminish. The mantle continues its secretions, though at a reduced rate; this tends to thicken the walls of the shell rather than to increase their size.

Ecology of Mollusks

Because mollusks are such a diverse group, there is hardly any environment, except the extreme polar regions, that does not support at least a few species. This widespread distribution is largely accounted for by the fact that mollusks have such a great capacity for adaptation. They live in the ocean to depths of 24,000 feet and in high mountain ranges at altitudes above 15,000 feet. They have been found in the arctic and antarctic zones, in deserts, caves, wells with a high salt content, mineral springs—in short, in many places where conditions for survival are extremely unfavorable.

Like all creatures, of course, they are most numerous where the environment favors their life style. And, in the case of the mollusks, this is the warm, damp belt around the world occupied by the tropical and temperate zones. Here, mollusks flourish not only in number and species but also in individual size and richness of ornamentation.

The gastropod Cypraea lurida *(below left) is a member of the cowrie family. Because of their beauty, cowrie shells have often been used as jewelry. In the South Pacific and in parts of Africa cowrie shells have been used as money.*

The common cuttlefish Sepia officinalis *(below) lives in the Mediterranean. It is sought for food, for its dark brown ink, and its internal shell. This shell, called cuttlebone, is used in the diet of cage birds because of its high calcium content.*

Since the distribution of the various species is related to the environment, scientists have been able to divide the seas and coasts and land areas of the world into molluscan "provinces." Each province is an area where given species are commonly found. Some provinces are broad indeed. The Indo-Pacific province, for example, includes the area from the coasts of eastern Africa, to southern Asia, north Australia, parts of India, and the Polynesian and Melanesian islands. Throughout this vast area the prevalent species of mollusks are quite similar to one another.

With some exceptions, the terrestrial mollusks prefer a damp habitat rich in humus and decaying plants, since these materials offer both a ready food supply and excellent hiding places. The mobility of land mollusks enhances their chances of survival. They can venture into inhospitable territories on hunting trips when food is in short supply and return again to their "resting" habitat.

Things are not so easy for fixed and semi-fixed mollusks, including the limpets and many bivalves. For them, finding a suitable habitat is imperative for survival. Some sessile species prefer to settle into sand or mud; others dig their way into rock or wood. Some

anchor themselves with a tangle of filaments. Still others survive as parasites, depending on living creatures such as jellyfish, sea anemones, corals, sea stars, sea urchins, and other mollusks.

A very special category of marine mollusks includes planktonic species. These animals have become adapted to life in the open sea, either on the surface or at shallow depths. Except for a few kinds of cephalopods these organisms are rarely equipped with a means of locomotion. They are at the mercy of the marine currents. As a result, their shells are very light, often glasslike, structures; some have no shell at all.

All mollusks have an affinity for water. Even the terrestrial species—and among them, even those that live in arid environments—must maintain a minimum degree of moisture around their bodies.

Temperature Cycles. In aquatic mollusks, the temperature of the water alone determines life cycles. But in land species, activity and rest are regulated by the amount of moisture available in the habitat or in the air. In almost all cases the passive period lasts longer than the active one, and especially when the climate is arid. Many land snails,

Once thought to be extinct, the genus Neopilina *(near right), was rediscovered in 1952.* Neopilina *is the only living member of the class* Monoplacophora.

A snail's foot (far right) has been photographed from beneath a sheet of glass. The bands on the bottom of the foot are caused by muscle contractions. These contractions move like an escalator from the front to the back of the foot.

for example, go through a daily cycle that is regulated by humidity. During the heat of the day they remain hidden, emerging only during the cooler hours, when dew descends. Rain disrupts this schedule, of course, and high humidity can bring the animals out even during the heat of the day.

The coming of cold weather always marks the onset of a period of hibernation for the terrestrial mollusk. Hibernation can last as long as six months. On the other hand, when summer weather is particularly hot and dry, some species go into a kind of summer lethargy called *estivation*. They seek coolness and dampness by various means, some digging holes almost 2 feet deep in the earth, where they may spend most of the summer.

General Habits

Because of the wide variety of body form and habitat among the mollusks, their methods of moving, feeding, and defense are also varied.

Locomotion. No animal group employs as many different methods of locomotion as the mollusks. Almost everyone has seen a land snail inching along, and every moviegoer has seen a thriller with an octopus swimming gracefully through the water or using its tentacles as legs to scramble across the sea bottom.

Not so well known are some of the species of marine gastropods that can leap about by springing with a strong, hooked foot. Some conchs can jump several inches. Other mollusks move from one place to another by burrowing through mud and sand. The gastropods dig with both head and body, while bivalves and tusk shells use their long, flexible foot.

The cephalopods are the best swimmers among mollusks. They use a system of jet propulsion, in which a stream of water is forced out of a siphon. Other groups manage

to swim about, too, if in a more rudimentary way. Certain bivalves, such as the scallop, swim in leaps by beating their valves rapidly, expelling a jet of water. Deep-sea gastropods move by means of vibrating cilia. And there is even a flying mollusk, called the sea arrow, or flying squid, which swims so rapidly that it often hurls itself 10 feet out of the water and has even landed on the decks of ships at sea.

Feeding Habits. Although the type of food preferred differs from one group to another, all mollusks that bear shells have a common requirement—their diet must be rich in calcium salts. Some mollusks are filter feeders, living on small particles of organic matter strained from the sea. Some are vege-

This distinctive scallop shell belongs to Pecten jacobaeus. *When attacked by predators, scallops attempt to escape by leaping away with a rapid closing of their valves.*

Most bivalves, such as the mussel Mytilus edulis *(right), spend their lives in an erect position on the edges of their shells. The two valves are of equal size. In contrast, oysters and scallops lie on one side since the lower valve is larger than the upper.*

A land slug Limax flavus *(below right) crawls on a mushroom. Members of this family, the Limacidae, often feed on mushrooms.*

tarians, others are carnivorous, and still others are scavengers.

Decaying organic matter is favored by many, and it is now certain that the dread shipworm ingests wood as well as boring into it. Bivalves draw in water and ingest everything that is suspended in it—diatoms, larvae, the eggs of small animals, etc. Elephant's-tusk shells devour Foraminifera and bivalve larvae that are common in the muddy bottoms where they live.

A large number of terrestrial snails are vegetarians, and may become real pests to farmers and gardeners. Among the marine mollusks, a plant diet seems to be limited to the more primitive forms, which have long and powerful radulae; the sea-going snails are carnivorous.

Among the carnivorous mollusks, the predatory octopus is an incorrigible hunter and displays great shrewdness when capturing its prey. In attacking large bivalves, it inserts a stone between the victim's valves to prevent them from closing. But this capacity for seemingly planned attack is not limited to the cephalopods. Some land snails dig underground tunnels to attack earthworms. Predatory marine snails use their proboscis, a tubelike extension from the head, to suck out the soft parts of their prey. Attack with a proboscis is usually so sudden that the victim, almost always a bivalve, may not have time to close itself within the safety of its shell. A large bivalve, however, can cause the snail's proboscis considerable damage by snapping shut its valves. For this reason, some snails insert a portion of their own shell between the open valves as a wedge before inserting the sucking tube.

If the bivalve should succeed in closing its valves and thwarting the initial attack, the hunter resorts to other means. Some swallow the prey whole if it is small enough, and grind it up in special stomachs. Some seize the bivalve with their foot and wait, with incredible patience, until it must either

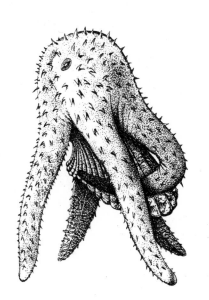

open its valves or suffocate. Others shatter the bivalve's shell with their own shell. Still others, called perforator mollusks, are capable of drilling a round hole in the victim's shell through which they suck out the contents. The genus *Conus*, a predatory gastropod, is perhaps the most sophisticated molluscan hunter of all. It has several tiny harpoons that carry a strong poison that quickly paralyzes the victim. The poison of several species is deadly to man.

Defense. Although the mollusks are, by and large, comparatively defenseless, some can offer extraordinary resistance to adverse conditions. One land snail lived for four years pasted to a library shelf in the British Museum, and another for six years imprisoned in a flask. This can be attributed to indefinitely prolonged hibernation, with a minimum consumption of energy.

When attacked by a predator, free-moving marine mollusks are not limited to the passive defense of hiding in their shells. Some bivalves, such as scallops, show surprising bursts of speed when fleeing their enemies. Some species also display autotomy —the ability to cast off body parts.

Often a snail will try to escape an enemy's notice by hiding under leaves. Marine mollusks may cover themselves with debris, stones, and dead shells, and may even attach these elements of camouflage to their shells. The nudibranch *Elysia viridis* is green when it is grazing on green algae, but turns orange when feeding on red algae.

Secretions form another line of defense. These range from jets of water, clouds of ink from the cephalopods, spurts of irritating and nauseous liquids, to expulsions of blood. As a last means of defense there is physical struggle. Some gastropods when seized will strike out with formidable blows of the foot, which is equipped with a sharp, menacing *operculum*, a horny plate that serves as a door to the shell. Under attack, the octopus

The sequence of pictures (above left) shows a cuttlefish as it captures a shrimp. In addition to its fixed arms, the cuttlefish has retractable tentacles that can shoot out rapidly to seize a victim. The fixed arms hold the prey while it is being eaten.

A starfish (below left) feasts on a bivalve. More than a hundred bivalves have been found in the stomach of a single starfish. Although most starfish only eat the soft parts of their prey, some starfish also injest the shell.

employs a series of increasingly intensive measures: flight, camouflage, hiding, mimicry, water jets, ink jets, offensive feints, self-mutilation, and—under extreme conditions—frantic blows with its strong beak.

The chief and most dangerous predators of marine mollusks are starfish, carnivorous snails, crabs, and fishes. Terrestrial species fall victim to various insects, frogs and other amphibians, reptiles, birds, rats, and, of course, man. And natural occurrences in an extreme degree—unusual variations in temperature and water salinity, floods, prolonged dry spells, and famine—can cause mass mortality in the mollusk population.

Longevity varies within a wide range. Some species of nudibranchs die in less than a year, while there are bivalves that apparently can live almost a century.

Longevity is partially determined, of course, by external factors—enemies, for one. Mollusks are attacked by many parasites, but these rarely cause death (cultivated oysters and mussels are an exception).

Mollusks and Man

From the beginning of time, people all over the world have valued mollusks for their usefulness. Oysters, clams, scallops, and mussels were among the first sources of food for prehistoric man. Remains of shells, sometimes huge mounds of them, may be found in all the ancient human settlements located on coastlines or next to bodies of fresh water. Today, oyster and clam fisheries provide employment for many thousands of men and women. Fleets of ocean-going vessels dredge for deep-sea scallops; others scoop clams from the muddy bottoms.

Practically all mollusks are edible. Some may be indigestible and some may have a nauseating taste, but none is in itself poisonous. Sickness that sometimes comes from eating mollusks and other seafood is often of an allergenic nature, or occurs as a result of bacterial contamination of mollusks taken from polluted waters. Hepatitis is one of the most serious diseases that can be contracted from eating seafood from polluted waters.

Also dangerous are mollusks that have swallowed certain dinoflagellate algae that are poisonous to man. Eating them can lead to paralysis and even death. Fortunately, however, the development of these algae requires special conditions that are comparatively rare.

Terrestrial mollusks are edible, too, and it is common practice in many countries to breed snails for the table. The tastiest species are considered to be *Helix pomatia* and *Helix aspersa*. Some smaller species are also eaten, but these usually are captured wild, since they do not breed well in captivity.

Early man probably first used shells as containers for water and other liquids. Even today in coastal areas of Greece people store olive oil in the capacious shells of *Tonna galea*, called the great tun, or helmet tun. Throughout history the large size, capacity, and shape of tun shells has earned them

"Blister pearls" are a mother-of-pearl covering formed in oyster shells over the tunnels of external borers, such as boring clams or worms. Pearls are produced when an irritant gets inside the mantle of an oyster. If unable to dislodge it, the oyster secretes a mother-of-pearl covering, which becomes the pearl. When a pearl is formed between the flesh and the shell, it may become overlain with additional mother-of-pearl and becomes an "attached pearl." Perfect spherical pearls are rarely formed in nature; most are odd shaped and are called "baroque pearls." They have little monetary value.

such popular and descriptive names as cask shells and wine jars.

Shells also served primitive man as tools—scrapers, blades, and awls. Strung together they become necklaces, bracelets, and belts, simple ornaments that are still worn today. Shells still have religious significance in some areas of Africa and the Indo-Pacific area, and in the Hindu religion the chank shell is sacred to the god Vishnu. Indeed, shells have had religious significance in many civilizations, serving as mystical symbols among certain ancient Greek, Roman, and Aztec sects.

Shells as Currency. One of the most interesting uses for shells, until fairly recent times, was as a form of money. *Cyprea moneta,* a small, oval, shiny, very common, and fairly attractive shell, was the widely used cowrie money of the South Pacific. Its use as legal tender spread to Arab and African tribes. Since its value in Africa was considerably greater than in the South Seas,

shipmasters made fortunes trading cheap goods for cowrie money in the Pacific islands and then exchanging the shells for valuable products in Africa. Even with inflated values there, it took a lot of shells to equal a dollar: from 20,000 to 100,000 shells to buy a slave; from 100,000 to 250,000 to buy a fine elephant tusk. With so many shells pouring in, African chiefs became cowrie millionaires and decorated everything—their canoes, their weapons, their wives, and themselves—with examples of their wealth.

Strangely enough, the Plains Indians of western North America also became cowrie addicts when someone discovered that the shells made good substitutes for elk's teeth, which were highly prized but becoming increasingly rare. The most common shell money among the Indians, however, especially those along the Pacific coast, was made from tusk shells of the genus *Dentalium.* Size and rarity combined to establish values, and a 6-foot string of the finest specimens was worth about $50.

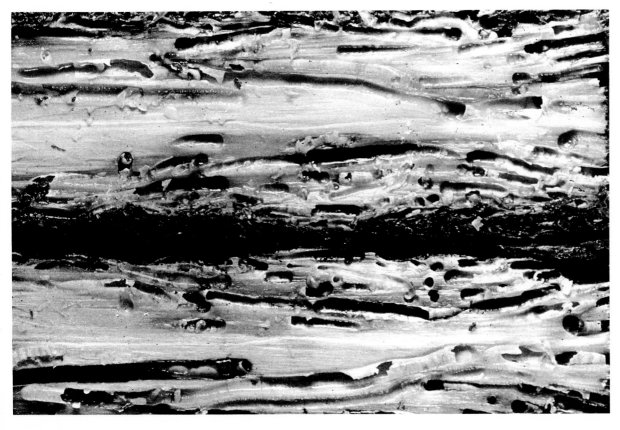

For centuries the shipworm, Teredo navalis, has been a waterfront pest, destroying wooden piers, wharves, and ships. Tiny larvae of these mollusks enter the wood. As they grow, they enlarge their passages, or galleries (left).

The wampum of the eastern Indians is probably the most familiar form of shell money. Wampum was made by cutting disks of white from whelk shells and disks of purple from quahog shells, stringing them on buckskin thongs, and rubbing them between grooved stones until the edges were smooth and almost perfectly round. Since the white shells were twice as easy to come by as the purple, a 6-foot string of white wampum was worth only half as much as a string of the purple.

Although shells are not used as money in our society, they still have great economic value. Mother-of-pearl buttons and other objects are made from the lustrous inner layers of *Pinctada*, *Turbo*, and *Trochus* shells, and exquisite cameos can be carved from the color-layered shells of various species. Even more important are the vast accumulations of shells that, gathered from beaches and dredged from the ocean bottom, are burned and crushed to make lime for agricultural use, and in some places are used to pave roads.

Pearls. In some mollusks, when a small, foreign body accidentally penetrates the space between the mantle and the shell, it causes an irritation and becomes covered by successive layers of nacre, or mother-of-pearl. When the irritating nucleus moves around, the coatings on it form a sphere that is not attached to the shell of the animal; the result is a pearl. Sometimes, however, the nucleus becomes attached to the shell.

Many bivalves form pearls. The most valuable pearls are produced by oysters of the genus *Pinctada*.

For many years the finest pearls came from fisheries in the Persian Gulf and the waters off Ceylon. But the natural-pearl industry suffered a severe setback about fifty years ago when a Japanese named Mikomoto developed the art of "seeding" *Pinctada* oysters with foreign bodies to force

the formation of pearls. Several years must pass before the pearl is ready for harvesting, but because the man who owns a "cultured" pearl farm is sure of his crop, he can afford to sell his wares for less than the natural-pearl diver, who must collect hundreds of oysters to find one containing a pearl of commercial value.

Cloth of Gold. Perhaps the most remarkable article obtained from seashells is a cloth woven from the byssus of a species of pen shell, *Pinna nobilis*, found in the Mediterranean. The byssus is a brushlike group of strong threads some bivalves secrete; they use it to anchor themselves to rocks and other rigid supports. The threads of the *Pinna* byssus have a metallic sheen, and cloth woven from them appears to be made of gold. The textile is so fine and soft that a scarf made of it can be passed through an ordinary finger ring. It is, as you might guess, very costly. Many historians believe that the golden fleece in the legend of Jason's adventures was probably made from the *Pinna* byssus.

Pigment. Anyone who has ever studied ancient history has heard of Tyrian purple dye, so expensive that only kings and emperors could afford cloth colored with it. This dye was obtained from the shells of several species of mollusks abundant in the Mediterranean. The process of extraction, once a closely guarded secret of the Phoenicians, consisted of soaking the shells in salt water, then boiling and straining the mixture until a clear pale-green pigment was obtained. Woolen cloth dipped into the solution and dried in the sun turned a muddy purple, but when washed with lye it took on gorgeous hues of crimson or magenta.

Another important pigment obtained from mollusks is sepia, the brownish ink secreted by some cephalopods, especially the cuttlefish. It is used in artists' colors.

Shells as Inspiration. Apart from practical uses, mollusk shells, in their infinite form, gracefulness, and beauty, have inspired sculptors, architects, and artists throughout history. The great architects of Greece immortalized shells in the ornamentation of their temples. The famous double-spiral staircase of the Chateau of Blois in France was probably inspired by the beautifully twisted core of the West Indian chank shell. The great 15th century Italian artist, Sandro Botticelli, painted Venus rising from the sea in a scallop shell. In fact, shell shapes have been used to ornament houses, jewelry, tableware, furniture, and works of art for many hundreds of years.

Collecting. The beauty of shells has turned many people into avid collectors. The passion for shells reached such heights in the 17th and 18th centuries that some collectors were quite prepared to squander their wealth to obtain particularly rare specimens. In the 19th century this interest became increasingly scientific, although it was aimed more at the shell then at the animal inside. The exquisitely rendered drawings illustrating a number of books published at that time have become collectors' items themselves.

Today the passion for shell collecting is on the rise again. There are several hundred clubs in the United States alone, and serious collectors are willing to spend large sums of money for the rarest and most beautiful shells. For the beginning collector, most public libraries have books on shells.

Unfortunately, many people take live mollusks for their shells; this has led to greatly decreased numbers of some of the most beautiful mollusks. This may also have harmful ecological effects. For example, the great recent increase in coral-eating starfish in some Pacific reefs has been blamed, by some ecologists, on the decrease of their natural enemy, the giant triton. Collectors avidly seek triton shells.

CLASS	SUBCLASS	ORDER	SUPERFAMILY
Monoplacophora			
Aplacophora		Neomenioidea Chaetodermatoidea	
Polyplacophora		Lepidopleurina Chitonina	
Bivalvia (Pelecypoda)	Paleotaxodonta		Nuculacea, Nuculanacea
	Cryptodonta		Solemyacea
	Pteriomorphia		Arcacea, Limopsacea, Mytilacea Pinnacea, Pteriacea, Pectinacea Anomiacea, Limacea, Ostreacea
	Paleoheterodonta		Unionacea, Trigoniacea
	Heterodonta		Lucinacea, Chamacea, Cyamiacea, Carditacea, Crassatellacea, Cardiacea, Tridacnacea Mactracea, Solenacea, Tellinacea Arcticacea, Dreissenacea, Glossacea, Corbiculacea, Veneracea, Myacea, Hiatellacea Pholadacea
	Anomalodesmata		Pandoracea, Clavagellacea, Poromyacea
Gastropoda	Prosobranchia	Archaeogastropoda	Pleurotomariacea, Fissurellacea Patellacea, Cocculinacea, Trochacea, Neritacea
		Mesogastropoda	Cyclophoracea, Valvatacea, Littorinacea, Rissoacea, Cerithiacea Epitoniacea, Eulimacea, Hipponicacea, Calyptraeacea, Strombacea, Cypraeacea, Atlantacea, Naticacea, Tonnacea
		Neogastropoda	Muricacea, Buccinacea, Volutacea, Conacea
	Opisthobranchia	Cephalaspidea Sacoglossa Anaspidea Thecosomata Gymnosomata Notaspidea Nudibranchia Gymnophila	
	Pulmonata	Basommatophora	Actophila, Amphibolacea, Siphonariacea, Hygrophila
		Stylommatophora	Veronicellacea, Succineacea, Tracheopulmonata, Achatinellacea, Pupillacea, Achatinacea, Oleacinacea, Endodontacea, Zonitacea, Acavacea, Bulimulacea, Helicacea, Streptaxacea
Scaphopoda			
Cephalopoda	Tetrabranchia		
	Dibranchia	Decapoda Octopoda Vampyromorpha	

Living Fossils— Monoplacophora

In 1952 a dredge being operated in the Pacific Ocean off Central America at depths greater than 10,000 feet brought to the surface two living species of the class Monoplacophora—a group that had been considered extinct. These mollusks, of the genus *Neopilina*, had been known only in fossil form dating back to the Cambrian and Devonian eras. The find was of great importance, for it enabled scientists to trace an evolutionary line between the development of mollusks and segmented marine worms of the phylum Annelida.

Members of *Neopilina* are about 1 inch long. The upper part of the animal is cov-

ered by a thin, circular shell with a curved top. A subcircular foot on the bottom is surrounded by a mantle groove in which five pairs of gills are symmetrically aligned. The mouth, or buccal cavity, is located in the front, and is equipped with tentacles mounted on stalklike structures. The radula has 40 to 45 rows of small teeth. Fertilization is external; the sexes are separate, and there are two pairs of gonads situated in the middle of the body. Just where fertilization takes place is unknown.

Little is known about the habits of these mollusks. The extreme thinness of the shell of the two known species, *N. galatheae* and *N. ewingi*, is undoubtedly due to the great depth at which they live. The comparative heaviness of the shells of fossil species suggests that the Monoplacophora once lived at shallower depths.

Crawling over submerged rocks and algae, most chitons eat plant material, which they scrape up with their mouth. In an intertidal zone (left) chitons stop feeding. They settle tightly against a rock, holding moisture under their shells. When the tide returns, the chitons become active again.

Wormlike Mollusks— Aplacophora

The members of the class Aplacophora are cylindrical, wormlike animals. In these primitive mollusks the head is indistinguishable from the body; and the foot, which is rudimentary, is hidden inside a ventral groove. In some, the foot is completely lacking. In place of a shell, the mantle produces calcareous spikes that protect the body.

The mouth is at the forward end and usually contains a radula. The alimentary tract is straight, the digestive apparatus terminating at a cavity in the hind end, which contains the anus, two kidney pores, and two gills. The circulatory and nervous systems are simple. Some species are her-maphroditic; others have separate sexes. The trochophoral larvae have dorsal plates until maturity.

There are only about 100 species in this group. They are cosmopolitan in their distribution and live on or near the sea bottom at depths ranging from a few to thousands of feet. Some species prefer muddy bottoms; others live with seaweeds and fixed sponges, possibly feeding off these organisms. The class is divided into two orders—the Chaetodermatoidea and the Neomenioidea.

In the Chaetodermatoidea there is one family, Crystallofrissonidae, which is divided into four genera with about a dozen species. These species have no ventral groove, but the head is marked by a transverse groove that separates it from the body. They are about 1 inch long. Predominantly found along northern coasts, *Prochaetoderma ra-*

duliferum, a member of this family, has been found in the Sea of Marmara in Turkey, where few other mollusks live.

The Neomenioidea are found primarily in northern regions, perhaps because that is where they have been most studied. The body is stumpy and slightly curved. The two ends are symmetrical, with the mouth and anal openings similarly placed. They have a ventral groove, and grow a keel on the dorsal surface. These hermaphroditic creatures are divided into three families, numerous genera, and many species.

Members of the family Lepidomeniidae have pedal grooves without distinct pedal folds and no gill folds, among other characteristics. The family Neomeniidae is comprised of neomenioids with gill folds in the anal chamber. The Proneomeniidae are neomenioids without gill folds but with pedal folds in the pedal groove.

Hiatella arctica is a bivalve that can drill tunnels into blocks of stone by rotating its very hard shell. Not even granite is immune to its steady boring.

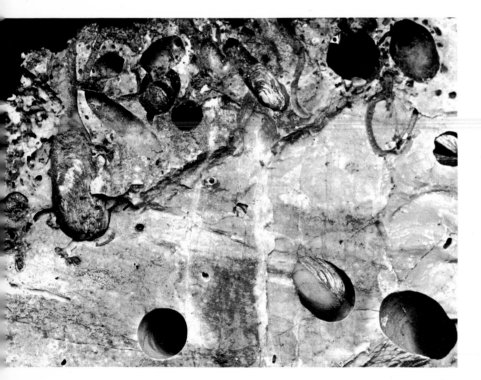

Chitons— Polyplacophora

Members of the class Polyplacophora are flattened and elongated, and are distinguished by a shell formed of eight transverse calcareous plates. Chitons range in length from less than 1 to more than 12 inches. Most are a dull shade of brown, green, red, or yellow. They are found in all parts of the world, usually in shallow water where their clinging powers prevent them from being washed from rocks by wave action. Some deep-water species have been dredged up from the ocean floor more than 12,000 feet down. They feed on algae and seaweeds, and are themselves eaten in the West Indies, where people pry them loose with thin knives and cook them into a dish known as "sea beef."

The eight-piece shell has bilateral symmetry. The six intermediate plates, similar to each other, overlap slightly. The front and rear plates are rounded on their outside edges. This system of plates gives the animal flexibility and enables it to curl up. The girdle juts out slightly all around the shell, securing the ends of the plates. It is protected by growths of spines, bristles, or scales. A long, flattened, and sturdy foot makes up the lower part of the body and is used both for movement and for holding to rocks.

At one end there is a mouth and a well-developed radula, although there is no real head. A short esophagus leads into the stomach, connected by ducts to a double liver. There is a long, coiled intestine that ends in an anus at the posterior end of the body.

Running along the sides of the body between the foot and the mantle is a groove that contains the gills. The number of pairs of gills present varies with the species from a few to more than fifty. The movement of threadlike cilia on the edges of the gills renews the water in the cavity.

The nervous system of the chiton is rudimentary, but it has special sense organs, known as "aesthetes," in definite clusters on the shell surface and connected to nerve filaments. In some species, the aesthetes act as light receptors, or eyespots. It is interesting to note, however, that chitons avoid light whenever possible.

The sexes are separate in these mollusks. Fertilization is external, and reproduction generally takes place in the spring or summer. When a male emits sperm in her vicinity, the female releases her eggs. In some cases the eggs are separate; in others they are held together by a gelatinous foam. The eggs may also be fixed to algae or rocks. The free-swimming larvae sink to the bottom before growing to maturity.

A study of *Chiton tuberculatus* by two investigators in 1919 verified what any casual observer of chitons would suppose— that chitons are exceedingly sluggish animals. The large specimen studied was attached to a concrete pier in Bermuda. During the nine months that it was observed, the animal stayed in an area of approximately six square feet. Often it remained immobile for a number of weeks. Of course, an adequate supply of food was available. Otherwise it probably would have been more active.

The present classification, based essentially on the shell, contains two orders: Lepidopleurina and Chitonina. The first order contains primitive, small species, and is divided into three families and numerous genera. The great majority of species (more than 400) belong to the order Chitonina, which includes more than ten families and many genera. They are particularly numerous in southern waters. The largest living species of the class is *Cryptochiton stelleri*, which is found in the North Pacific.

Clams, Oysters, And Others— Bivalvia

The class Bivalvia includes many of the most familiar and widely eaten mollusks— oysters, clams, scallops, and mussels. All members of this group have two valves, or shells. With more than 10,000 species, the bivalves are one of the largest classes of mollusks. This class is also known as the Pelecypoda, meaning "hatchet foot."

Bivalves are found in salt, brackish, or freshwater habitats. None are terrestrial. The bivalves are generally rather sedentary in their habits. They are found mainly on soft bottoms, and are well-adapted for burrowing in sand and mud. Some are specially adapted for boring into hard surfaces. Most are filter feeders, existing on small particles

Much of our knowledge of the earth's history has been provided by fossils, including fossils of bivalves. The fossil (below) of the clam Megalodon gumbeli *was formed during the Triassic period, some 200 million years ago.*

of organic material that are obtained from the sea water.

An interesting characteristic of bivalves is their ability to produce silt. They secrete large quantities of mucus that collects in a mass the sand, minerals, and organic particles that are carried into the mantle cavity with the sea water. This agglutinized mass of material is periodically eliminated, and it helps to form marine mud. Oysters produce about 1 gram of silt a day, and in the neighborhood of oyster banks, the accumulation assumes enormous proportions over a period of time.

The Shells. The shells of bivalves are hinged together at the top by a strong elastic ligament. The animal closes the valves by contracting a pair of powerful muscles called the anterior and posterior *adductor muscles*. The hinge ligament exerts its force in the opposite direction from the adductor muscles. Thus, when the adductor muscles are relaxed, the pull of the hinge ligament opens the shells. In oysters and scallops there is only a posterior adductor muscle; however, it is more centrally located.

The two shells are generally oval in shape and heavily calcified. In most groups they are similar to each other in size and shape. However, in some sessile families, one valve is larger than the other. On the dorsal surface of each shell is a knoblike structure called the *umbo*. This protuberance is the oldest part of the shell, and around it can be seen concentric growth lines.

The shells of bivalves vary tremendously in size—in some freshwater forms they are less than $\frac{1}{10}$ inch in length, while the shells of the giant clam may be more than 4 feet long and weigh 500 pounds. The shells also exhibit great variety in color and shape.

The Mantle. In the bivalves the mantle is divided into two lobes that completely enclose the soft parts of the animal. Each lobe of

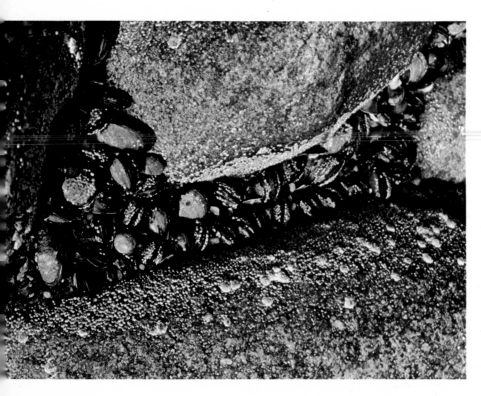

the mantle secretes a shell. In the dorsal part of the body the mantle covers the visceral mass and hangs down like a skirt. The large mantle cavity is found between the ventral edges of the two lobes of the mantle and the visceral mass.

The ventral edges of the lobes of the mantle may be partially joined together. However, there is an opening for the foot and two smaller posterior openings to allow water to circulate through the cavity. Water carrying food and oxygen enters through one opening, while water containing wastes passes out of the animal through the other.

In many bivalves the mantle lobes extend outward in the form of siphons, which perform the same functions as the two openings described above. The edges of the mantle often contain sense organs.

The Foot. The bladelike foot is used for burrowing by most bivalves. In some, however, it is used for locomotion—either leaping,

The typical shape and shell pattern of the ribbed mussel Modiolus demissus *(above) can be seen on this cleaned specimen. In their natural habitat (left), these mussels are partially buried in silt and mud; their shells are encrusted with barnacles.*

31

creeping, or swimming. In the mobile mollusks and those that bury in mud and sand, the foot is robust and highly developed.

Movement of the foot depends on the action of muscles running from the foot to the shell and on hydrostatic pressure in the foot. This pressure is produced both by the blood and by water in the mantle cavity. The foot is extended by increasing the blood pressure in it, and by the contraction of a pair of protractor muscles. It is retracted by the contraction of retractor muscles; in retracting the foot the blood leaves it and passes back into the mantle cavity or sinuses.

In groups such as the oysters, which lead fixed or sedentary lives, the foot is reduced in size. Mussels, which are sessile bivalves, attach themselves to the substratum by strong threads called the *byssus*, which is secreted by a gland in the foot. In making the attachment, the foot is extended to the substratum. The byssus runs down the foot to the substratum. On exposure to water the byssus hardens to form tough filaments.

Mussels are the most common and most abundant of the bivalves. Their dense colonies can be found both in salt water and in rivers, clinging to rocks or other hard objects.

Internal Anatomy. Bivalves have one pair of gills, although in some groups the gills are folded in such a way that there appear to be two pairs on each side of the body. The beating of cilia on the gill surfaces keeps water circulating through the body cavity. In sessile animals, this water current brings food as well as a constant supply of oxygen.

Thus, the gills have become the main food-getting organ in most bivalves. They have become anatomically specialized for separating food particles—generally tiny planktonic plants—from the water. The particles become entangled in mucus on the gill surface, and the food-laden mucus is passed along ciliated food grooves to the mouth. The cilia and grooves of the gills also sort particles by size so that those entering the mouth are not too large. Around the mouth are leaflike projections called *labial palps*, which help push food into the mouth.

The mouth opens into a short esophagus, which in turn empties into a large stomach. The stomach is connected by ducts to the liver, a gland that produces digestive enzymes. The liver is the site of absorption. Following the stomach is a winding intestine, which terminates in the rectum and anus.

The gills are the major site of respiration, although some exchange may take place at the inner surface of the mantle. In a few species the mantle is the main site

of respiration, and the gills are degenerate.

In a bivalve, the blood is pumped through the body by the contraction of the muscular ventricle of the heart. From the ventricle the blood passes into two arteries that end in sinuses in the tissues. From there it passes through the two kidneys, or nephridia, and into the gills, where it releases carbon dioxide and picks up oxygen. From the gills the blood passes back to the heart.

Excretion of liquid wastes is carried out by the pair of nephridia, which are located near the chamber containing the heart.

The nervous system consists of three pairs of ganglia and two pairs of nerve cords. The cerebropleural ganglia are on either side of the esophagus; the visceral ganglia are near the posterior adductor muscle; and the pedal ganglia are in the foot.

The edible mussel Mytilis edulis *extends its foot to discharge a byssus, which is a bundle of tough protein threads. This can be used to secure the animal to rigid submerged structures, or it can be extended briefly to provide temporary anchorage.*

Most of the sense organs in bivalves are along the edge of the mantle. These include touch receptors and chemoreceptors, as well as ocelli (simple eyes). There is a pair of statocysts in the foot near the pedal ganglia.

Another sense organ, the *osphradium,* is located beneath the posterior adductor muscle. It may be involved in chemoreception.

The sexes are separate in the bivalves, and in most species, except for those that brood their eggs, fertilization takes place in the water. In marine bivalves, the embryo develops first into a free-swimming torchophore larva and then into a veliger larva. In the veliger larva the ciliated crown shows the first signs of an unpaired dorsal shell. Following the formation of the mantle, the adult shells develop; growth into a mature individual occurs gradually.

Bivalves of the Past

One of the oldest known genera is *Lamellodonta,* from the Middle Cambrian of Spain. Although they are not as old as the gastropods, the bivalves are a very ancient group of mollusks. Among early bivalvian groups were *Ctenodontha* and *Modiolopsis,* genera that lived from the Ordovician period to the Silurian. *Ctenodonta* occurred in North America, while the genus *Modiolopsis* was cosmopolitan in distribution. An interesting genus was *Ambonychia,* a mussel-like clam that ocurred in the Middle to Upper Ordovician of North America and Europe. Actually, many of the names formerly applied to Paleozoic clams are no longer used other than as collective names for groups of clams. The rudistids are one such group.

The extinct *Hippurites*, one of the rudistids, is interesting for the heated discussions it once caused among paleontologists seeking to assign the genus to a systematic position. These animals, which lived at the end of the Mesozoic era and disappeared about 65 million years ago, fixed themselves by one valve to a solid structure under water, usually a rock. The fixed valve became long and curved until it looked like a horn; the second valve became smaller and smaller.

Confronted by this extremely uncommon form, scholars debated long and hard. Finally, after a great deal of research, they agreed that the rudistids formed a group of bivalves, characterized by a special hinge, whose shell had evolved into highly unequal valves as a result of adaptation to rocky environments. The classification is based in part on the manner in which the shell was fixed to the substratum, and in part on the structure of the shell itself.

An old name given to this extinct group, Pachyodonta, applies to a large, conical tooth on the smaller valve. An indentation at the base of the tooth accommodated the anterior adductor muscle, and the tooth itself was neatly fitted into an ample hollow in the large, fixed valve. The arrangement forms what is known as a "pachydont hinge" —*pachy* meaning "thick," and *odont* meaning "tooth."

Barnacles and sea worms encrust the valves of these mussels. When cleaned, these mussels are easily recognized as Mytilus galloprovincialis, *a blue mussel that lives in the Mediterranean Sea.*

shells. In the nut shells the small valves are triangular, and the hinge is provided with many fine teeth. The teeth, found on both valves, interlock so perfectly with each other that it is almost impossible to reclose the shell after the valves have been separated.

The inside of the shell is lined with mother-of-pearl; the outside is thick, horny, and the color of dirty sand. Lack of bright colors is typical of deep-water species, and although some Nuculidae may be found in shallow waters, they range down to depths of 4,000 feet. The genus *Nucula* is one of the most common of the family.

The Nuculanacea. The superfamily Nuculanacea is closely related to the Nuculacea, but has no mother-of-pearl on the inside of the valves. The shells are elongated, and sometimes extend into a pointed beak. These mollusks are inhabitants of cold, deep waters, particularly in the Arctic. Common genera include *Nuculana* and *Yoldia*.

Bivalves of the genus Pinna *(left) have the largest mollusk shells in the Mediterranean. Members of this genus also have the unique ability to stand upright in the sand. Sometimes more than two feet high, they are secured in their position by a byssus—a bundle of protein threads. Each thread is attached to a sand particle.*

A valve of a young Pinna nobilis *(below) is covered with thin, upright scales. The byssuses of these bivalves have been used to weave a strong, light, beautiful textile that is called "cloth-of-gold."*

The Paleotaxodonta

The subclass Paleotaxodonta contains primitive mollusks with gills composed of simple, unbent filaments and with highly developed labial palps. The intestine is long and twisted, the nervous system rudimentary and incomplete. The elongated foot is formed for creeping. The taxodont shell, composed of numerous teeth, has equal valves that are serrated at the edges; the inside of some is layered with mother-of-pearl. The adductor muscles are of roughly equal size.

The Nuculacea. The superfamily Nuculacea is represented in all the seas of the world. It includes the family Nuculidae, the nut

The Cryptodonta

The subclass Cryptodonta includes mollusks that have shells in which the teeth are totally, or almost totally, nonexistent. The shell has two equal valves and is generally round and thin. The anterior adductor muscle is narrower and much longer than the posterior muscle. Well-adapted for burrowing in sand, the foot is long and slender. In their other characteristics these animals are similar to the Paleotaxodonta.

The Solemyacea. The superfamily Solemyacea is a group with only a few species scattered in various seas. The valves of the shell are devoid of teeth. They are held together by a thick, smooth, elastic membrane that extends beyond the valves themselves. This *periostracum* is dark brown in color, and is marked by radial lines that give the mollusk a readily recognizable appearance.

The family Solemyidae has only a few genera other than *Solemya. S. velum*, which ranges from Nova Scotia to Florida, has delicate, yellowish-brown shells. A brown epidermis hangs down like a veil. This species, which is about 1 inch long, lives buried in the sand.

S. borealis is a smiliar species, but it is about 2 inches long and tan colored. It is less widely distributed than *S. velum*, being found from Nova Scotia only to southern New England.

The Pteriomorphia

In members of the subclass Pteriomorphia the shell hinge may be of several types: it may have a large number of teeth; there can be one large tooth with a hollow on the corresponding valve; or there can be greatly reduced double teeth. The mantle cavity is lacking.

The Arcacea. The superfamily Arcacea is a very important one with more than 200 species, which are found in all the seas of the world. Members of this group are commonly known as ark shells or box shells because of the box- or shiplike appearance of their shells.

Ark shells attach themselves firmly to rocks by byssal filaments. The dark color and roughness of their valves provide them with excellent camouflage.

In the ark shell, the foot is large, pointed, and has a lobe reminiscent of a heel. The posterior end has one opening shaped like a figure eight, instead of two separate openings or siphons. There are two hearts, and the blood in some species is red. Members of the genus *Arca* are commonly known as blood clams because of their red blood.

Noah's ark shell, *Arca noae,* is found in shallow waters in the Mediterranean. The similar zebra ark shell, or turkey wing, *Arca zebra,* occurs in the western Atlantic, from North Carolina south to Brazil. The heavy shell of these species is elongated and almost quadrangular in shape. It may be up to 4 inches long. The hinge is composed of a line of about 50 teeth. The shell has ridges radiating out from the umbo and is striped with brown and yellow. Along the edge of the mantle is a series of ocelli.

The blood ark shell, *Anadara ovalis,* is found in shallow water along the east coast of the United States. The shell is ovoid and up to 3 inches in length. The outside is dark brown and shaggy.

The ponderous ark shell, *Noetia ponderosa,* is about 2 inches long and is found from Virginia to Texas. The upper parts of the valves are almost white, but the lower parts are dark brown and furry.

The Limopsacea. The superfamily Limopsacea includes bivalves in which the shell is almost perfectly circular. Like the ark shell, however, it has a large number of teeth.

Thorny oysters of the genus Spondylus *occur in warm waters around the world. The Mediterranean thorny oyster S. gaederopus (above) is heavily camouflaged with sponge and growths. When cleaned, the shell has a lavender upper valve and a white lower valve.*

The great scallop Pecten maximus *(left) is common along the Atlantic coast of Europe. It reaches a diameter of 5 inches.*

There are two families in this group—the Limopsidae, in which the shell is tiny, and the Glycymeridae, in which the shell is very large. The limopsids are inhabitants of cold seas, living on muddy bottoms, sometimes at considerable depths.

The glycymerids, with about 60 species, are more widespread and can be found in warmer waters. One species, *Glycymeris glycymeris,* lives in Mediterranean sands at a shallow depth. It is sometimes sold in fish markets, but the meat is leathery and not much appreciated.

Glycymeris pennaceus has rounded valves a little over 1 inch in diameter. This species is found along the southeastern coast of the United States and in the West Indies. Lines on the shell make it look like a grid. The foot is cresent-shaped.

The Mytilacea. The mussels of the superfamily Mytilacea are the most common bivalves. They are found in all temperate and cold seas. Mussels are eaten in many parts of the world. Some live in rivers, but most species are marine. "Their elongate, narrowed shells," writes Roy Waldo Miner in his *Field Book of Seashore Life,* "are found on the shores of all continents. They hang in masses on wharf timbers. They cover mud flats with a continuous carpet, and all stationary or floating objects near the low-tide mark and for some distance between the tides, on rocky cliffs. They invade barnacle and oyster beds, and, in the latter respect, are a problem to fishermen. In European countries, they are an important source of food and so form the basis of a profitable industry. This would, doubtless, also be true in our own country were not oysters much more profitable and desirable here."

The practice of breeding mussels, a form of aquaculture, in Europe dates back to Roman times, and today is valuable not only for economic reasons but also because it insures that the mollusks brought to market are free of parasites and bacterial contamination. The ideal environment for mussel breeding is water that is agitated rather than stagnant, rich in phytoplankton (tiny planktonic plants), and, of course, unpolluted. Periodic checks on the purity of the water are important. When these ideal conditions are met, breeders can grow healthy mussels that are considerably larger than those born in the wild.

The common edible mussel is *Mytilus edalis.* It is found in large numbers along both coasts of the Atlantic. It is also found north to arctic waters and as far south in the Pacific as northern California.

The shells of edible mussels are usually a dark color, brown, blue, or almost black, and the interior lining is often pearly. They are usually about 3 inches long. The cylindrical foot spins a coarse, hairy byssus that has great clinging power. Sexes are separate. The soft parts of the male are yellowish; those of the female are brick red.

Other common genera of this superfamily are *Modiolus* and *Lithophaga.* Members of the genus *Modiolus* are similar to mussels of the genus *Mytilus,* but some species have a fringe on the shell. *Lithophaga* is notable for its ability to burrow perfectly circular holes into rock. *Lithophaga lithophaga,* the sea date, is prized in the Mediterranean for its excellent flavor.

Tiny pinpoints of blue mark the eyes along the edge of the mantle of this St. James scallop (below, left).

A freshwater mussel of the genus Anodonta *(below right) has a thin, elliptical shell. A number of species occur in freshwater streams and lakes of North America and Eurasia.*

The file shell Lima in-flata *(left) can move swiftly in the water. It swims backwards, trailing its colorful tentacles behind. It can also crawl backwards, with its foot protruding from between the rounded margins of the shell.*

The Pinnacea. Members of the superfamily Pinnacea are commonly known as the pen shells. They are large bivalves with fragile, wedge-shaped shells. They are generally found sunken to about a quarter of their length into sand, with the pointed, anterior end down, and solidly anchored by a long, strong byssus.

The part of the pen shell that is thrust into the sand is lined with a very thin layer of mother-of-pearl. Pen shells can form pearls. In some species the pearls are brightly colored but valueless; in others they are black and of some value.

The valves of pen shells are fastened by large adductor muscles. The muscles of

some species, such as *Atrina serrata* of the southeastern United States, are sold as large scallops. The meat of other species is edible but extremely tough. Pen shells found along the coasts of eastern North America sometimes grow to 1 foot in length. They cannot compare, however, with *Pinna nobilis* of the Mediterranean, which sometimes has shells more than 27 inches in length.

The Pteriacea. The superfamily Pteriacea includes the famous pearl oysters of the genus *Pinctada*. They have been avidly sought throughout history for the beautiful and valuable pearls they sometimes contain. Edible oysters do not belong to this group,

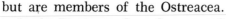

A file shell of the species **Lima inflata** *rests on the sea floor (below). Its tentacles cover its partially open, white valves.*

Scallops are agile swimmers. Two scallops (bottom) dart through the water by beating their valves. Other scallops and a starfish rest on the bottom.

but are members of the Ostreacea.

In the Pteriacea the valves are of unequal size, with the right one on which the animal rests being smaller. This valve is attached to the substratum by the byssus. The larger valve may be almost 12 inches in length. Members of this group, which includes the wing shells as well as the pearl oysters, are found in temperate and tropical seas throughout much of the world.

The best-known species of pearl oysters are *Pinctada margaritifera* and *P. maxima*. They are most commonly found in large coastal banks at depths of from 30 to 250 feet. They have a wide distribution and are found in the Red Sea, the Indian Ocean, and the South Pacific, with smaller relatives in the Caribbean.

One of the oldest, still-productive pearling areas is around the island of Ceylon in the Indian Ocean. Some of the finest pearls come from the Persian Gulf. While hundreds of millions of pearl oysters are gathered during the pearling season, only a tiny per cent

of them yield pearls, and of these, only a relative few of gem quality.

Cultured pearls are produced by inserting a bead made of mother-of-pearl between the mantle and the shell of a pearl oyster. The bead then becomes covered with a thin layer of nacre.

The Atlantic wing shell, *Pteria colymbus*, is a relative of the pearl oyster. This 4-inch mollusk, marked with brown, triangular spots on radiating bands of white, ranges from the southeastern United States to the West Indies.

Other members of the Ptericea include the comparatively few tropical species of the family Malleidae, notable for the shapes of their shells. One of them, *Malleus malleus*, resembles a hammer.

The Pectinacea. The superfamily Pectinacea includes the common edible scallop and its relatives. The edible scallop, *Pecten irradians*, is the most common scallop along the east coast of North America. Only the

large and tender adductor muscle—there is only one—is eaten in many countries, but in the West Indies and South America the entire animal is eaten.

The superfamily Pectinacea is divided into two principal families—Pectinidae and Spondylidae. Their shells come in a seemingly endless variety of colors and patterns, and the beautiful ornamentation makes them prize catches for eager shell collectors.

In the Pectinidae the valves are unequal in size. They are rounded but come to a point at the umbo. On each side of the umbo is a rather large wing. The foot is cylindrical. There are no siphons. On the mantle of the pectens is a continuous row of 30 to 40 bright blue eyes.

The Pectinidae include hundreds of species found in all seas. Most species are free-moving, although the young sometimes live attached to the substratum by a byssus. Adult scallops swim by opening and closing their valves with great force. This expels a jet of water that moves the scallop through the water.

Argopecten irradians is usually 2 to 3 inches in diameter. The color varies but usually includes shades of white, gray, yellow, brown, red, and orange. The shell has less than 20 wide ribs radiating from the umbo. This scallop is found from New England to the Gulf of Mexico, often on mud flats or in eel grass.

Placopecten magellanicus, the giant, or deep sea, scallop, may be more than 6 inches in length. Unlike the common scallop, its shell has no wide ribs. The upper valve is brown and convex, while the lower valve, which is white, is almost flat. The wings on the shell are equal in size. This scallop is found from the middle-Atlantic states north to Labrador.

Chlamys islandicus is found from New England north to the Arctic and off the coasts of northern Europe. It is 2½ to 3 inches in diameter. The valves are roughly

The edible oyster Ostrea edulis *is a favorite dish of gourmets. The ancient Chinese and the Romans bred oysters. Modern oyster breeding is an important economic activity, but pollution of offshore waters has endangered oyster beds in many countries.*

equal in size, but the wings are not. There are more than 50 narrow ribs radiating from the umbo. It is brightly colored, with bands of purple, pink, red, and orange.

Members of the family Spondylidae have strong heavy shells. The shells are armed with scales or spines that are sometimes contorted and very long, especially on the upper valve. The smaller, lower valve is usually fixed to a rock. These shells are not rare, but are difficult to obtain in good condition. Some tropical specimens, which are beautifully colored and sculptured, are in great demand and sell for high prices.

The Limacea. Members of the superfamily Limacea are known as file shells because the ridges of their valves consist of pointed, overlapping scales. They are closely related to the scallops. Their shells are yellowish or white in color, somewhat oval in shape, and equal in size. The mantle has a fringe at the border and is set with little eyes.

These mollusks can be seen swimming about in schools, zigzagging with the abruptness of scallops as they open and close their valves. They travel hinge foremost, trailing behind them a flowing, graceful sheaf of long mantle tentacles, which in some species are colored a brilliant orange, pink, or rose. Sometimes they throw these long filaments about each other and swim by twos and threes. When drawn in, these fringes become somewhat rigid and protect the valves.

Some species of file shells prefer to remain stationary, and build nests from webs of byssal threads plastered with slime and stuccoed with bits of shell, coral, seaweed, and pebbles. The whole nest is attached to the roots of large seaweeds. Several young will often be found occupying the same nest, but adults are always solitary. Nests are funnel shaped, and wide enough to permit the mollusk to move up and down but not to turn around.

The little porcelain crab lives in the nest of the gaping file shell, *Lima hians*, of the British Isles and the Mediterranean, with the full consent of the owner. It probably acts as a scavenger, keeping the house clean in return for its lodging.

A Cardium tuberculatum, one of the cockles or heart shells, displays the large, strong foot that enables the animal to bury itself in sandy or muddy bottoms.

Limacea is an old group, and includes more than 300 fossil forms from the Carboniferous period, from 350 to 275 million years ago. The living species are found chiefly in cold or temperate seas.

Lima scabra is found along the southeastern coast of the United States and in the Caribbean. The shell is yellow-colored and oval, with scalloped edges. These file shells may be up to 5 inches in length.

The Anomiacea. Members of the superfamily Anomiacea are commonly called jingle shells because if you shake a pail of them, they clink musically. Although the shells are dainty and look fragile, they do not break easily. The species range in color from pale shades of yellow, salmon, and silver to bluish-black. Sometimes called golden shells, they are among the most familiar and abundant shells on the eastern and southern beaches of the United States.

A popular pastime of years gone by was to string these little shells and hang them, curtainlike, in the windows and doorways of seaside cottages. Other hobbyists pierced them near the hinge and made strings to drape over lampshades.

The shells used for these purposes, as well as those washed up on the beaches, are almost always the jingle shell's upper valve. The lower valve is smaller and has a large hole near the hinge through which the animal sends out a very strong calcified byssus. Early in life, using this byssus, members of the common genus *Anomia*, as well as other jingle shells, attach themselves to some rough surface. So firmly does the mollusk cling that the lower valve often becomes deformed during growth, and assumes the shape of its support. When it adheres to a scallop, for example, its surface molds itself to conform to the sculpture and ornamentation of its host.

The need to anchor is so strong that jingle shells will pile upon each other if no other support is available, each firmly riveting itself to the one below. Oyster dredges often bring up masses of them alive, their shells all ajar. A tap on one of the outer shells causes it to close tight; then, like dominoes falling, the signal is passed down the line until all snap shut.

Anomia is a small genus but widely distributed. It was named by Carolus Linnaeus, the 18th century Swedish naturalist, who decided that they should be called *anomia*, or "nameless," since no descriptive name was possible for shells that changed their form to fit the objects on which they grew.

Residents of the Philippine Islands sometimes use the large, flat, translucent valves of the genus *Placuna* as a substitute for glass, building them into walls in the form of windows.

The Ostreacea. The superfamily Ostreacea includes the edible oysters. There are 5 genera with about 50 species in this group.

The clam Tridacna maxima *(top and left) has a beautiful blue mantle, though coloration varies among individual specimens. The bivalve is an inhabitant of coral reefs in the western Pacific.*

The giant clam, Tridacna gigas *(bottom), is fairly common along the Great Barrier Reef of Australia. Due to its size, exaggerated stories describe it as a menace to divers, who may accidently put a hand or foot inside its massive, powerful valves. The valves close slowly, however, and it would probably be difficult to be caught by the so-called "man-trap-clam."*

Oysters are one of the most popular seafood delicacies. They are also the raw material for a very important industry. Oyster breeding was practiced by the ancient Romans and probably even earlier by the Chinese. In Europe, *Ostrea edulis*, the edible oyster, is the favored species, but in North America the larger *Crassostrea virginica*, the Virginia or American oyster, is considered the most valuable commercially.

Oysters have think heavy shells that are unequal in size. The oyster lives permanently attached by the larger shell to some hard object. The surface of the dark gray shells is very rough and uneven. There is no foot. There is only one adductor muscle. Members of the genus *Ostrea* are found in all but the coldest seas.

Crassostrea virginica is extremely abundant along the Atlantic coast, and has been transplanted to the Pacific. The larger commercially bred specimens may reach 3 to 4 inches in length; 6-inch specimens are fairly common, and individuals that are 12 inches or more in length have been found.

In this species the sexes are separate. Reproduction takes place during the summer months. The oysters are not dangerous to eat during this period, but are less tasty—a fact that accounts for the belief that they should not be consumed during months without the letter "r" in the name. The eggs or sperm are carried in the mantle in a milky fluid that is discharged into the sea. It is estimated that a large female oyster produces more than 50 million eggs at a time.

Fertilization takes place in the sea. Within a few days the fertilized eggs hatch into trochophore larvae. Many larvae are washed out to sea, and many more are eaten by other sea creatures. The millions that remain, giving the water a cloudy appearance, swim freely for only a day or two. They then develop into veliger larvae and settle down on some hard object to which they attach themselves for life. Ideal anchoring spots are on or near empty shells that, in disintegrating, add lime to the water; the young oyster, remember, must have lime to build its thick shell.

Under good conditions, the oyster adds about an inch to its shell each year of its life for the first 10 years. Thereafter its growth goes into thickening the shell, rather than adding to its circumference. Full reproductive power comes after about 4 years, although spawning usually begins earlier. Growth generally occurs during the summer, with the winter spent in comparative hibernation. Layers of the shell mark periods of growth, but do not equate with age. Oysters are considered to have a life-span of about 10 years, but the size and thickness of the shells of animals that are known to have lived relatively undisturbed in rich feeding grounds suggest a possible extreme age of over 50 years.

In addition to man, oysters are widely preyed upon by other animals. The starfish, for example, is a notorious predator of oysters and destroyer of oyster beds. Prying the valves apart, the starfish turns its stomach inside-out and inserts it inside the oyster's shell. It then digests the soft parts of the oyster and withdraws its stomach.

The Paleoheterodonta

Members of the subclass Paleoheterodonta, like the Heterodonta, are found either lying on the bottom sand or mud or burrowed in it; however, these forms are generally not attached.

The Trigoniacea. Most of the Trigoniacea are extinct. The living members of this group include only a few species of the genus *Neotrigonia*, which are found in Australia.

The Unionacea. The superfamily Unionacea is a vast and important group of freshwater clams. They inhabit the sandy and muddy bottoms of streams and ponds on every continent. Pearls produced by these mollusks once were sought by man, but the introduction of cultured pearls has reduced their value. Some species are eaten, and the shells of others are used to make mother-of-pearl buttons.

In these clams, the dark-colored valves are of equal size, and there is a large foot. Eggs are hatched in brood pouches located in the gills of the parent; the young stay in the brood pouch until they hatch into glochidia larvae. When discharged, they lie on the bottom with their byssal cords floating upwards. To survive, they use the byssus to hitch a ride on a passing fish. They live as parasites on the fish until their vital organs are fully developed.

The Heterodonta

In bivalves of the subclass Heterodonta the lobes of the mantle are usually joined together, and in most there are two siphons. The hinge of the shell is equipped with cardinal teeth—three at most—on each valve, all of which are different from each other. In addition to the cardinal teeth, which are central, the valves generally are fitted with a number of scalelike lateral teeth.

The Lucinacea. Members of the superfamily Lucinacea have round shells that are of equal size. In some the shells are quite fragile. These bivalves are generally found burrowed in sandy and muddy bottoms. In some families of the Lucinacea there are no siphons, while in others there is only an excurrent siphon. In all groups the foot is used to construct the tube through which water enters the burrow.

The genus *Lucina* is a large one, with

about 100 species. In some the foot is twice as long as the animal. Most of these bivalves are very small and white. *Phacoides nuttalli* is found along the Pacific coast of Mexico and southern California. It is about 1 inch in length. *Phacoides filosus* occurs in

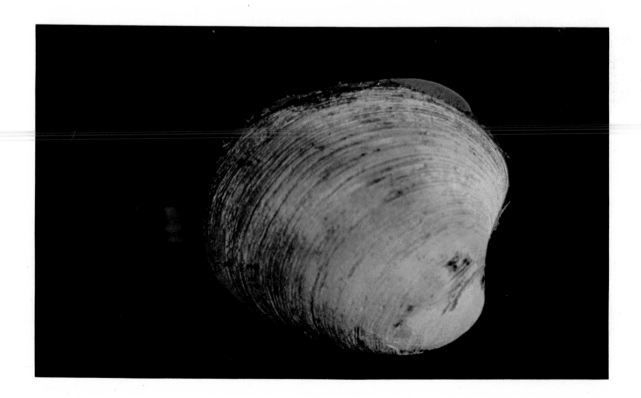

moderately deep water from the arctic regions to the Gulf States. It is about 1½ inches long.

The Chamacea. The superfamily Chamacea has only three living genera, although there are many known fossil genera. Members of the genus *Chama*, the best-known genus, are characterized by shells with a rather irregular outline and surface; externally, they are wrinkled, spiny, or scaly. The foot is greatly reduced. The animal fixes itself to a rocky substratum by means of one of the valves, which then becomes almost like a part of the rock to which it is joined. The fixed valve may be either the right or the left one, but each member of a given species always uses the same valve. The free valve is the smaller of the two, and in appearance is almost like a small lid, well hinged with strong teeth.

The Carditacea. Members of the superfamily Carditacea have heart-shaped or oval shells that are often ornamented with large radial ribs and sometimes also by scales. These marine bivalves have a foot and byssus.

Beguina calyculata, a Mediterranean dweller, is outstanding by virtue of its elongated form and the bizarre ornamentation on its shell.

Some of the species of *Cardita* found in tropical waters—*Cardita crassicosta* from the Indian Ocean is one example—are considered great treasures by collectors because of their splendidly ornamented shells.

Venericardia borealis, the northern heart shell, is found from North Carolina to Labrador. The shell is dark brown and about 1 inch in length.

The Crassatellacea. Members of the superfamily Crassatellacea are found in the deepest parts of the temperate seas, and at shallower depths in colder bodies of water. They are small bivalves shaped like rounded triangles. Their shells are often ornamented

The quahog, or hardshell, clam Mercenaria mercenaria *(left) usually lies partially buried in the sand or silt of the sea bottom. When mature, it is about 5 inches in length. When half-grown, it is called a "cherrystone" and is one of the most flavorful of clams.*

by concentric grooves. The color of the shell is usually a shade of brown, like the mud in which they live. Because of the solidity and shape of their valves, they are sometimes called thick-shelled hearts.

Some of the most common members of this group belong to the genus *Astarte*. *A. sulcata* is sometimes dredged up from a 6,000-foot depth in the Mediterranean. *A. borealis* ranges from New England to the Arctic Ocean. These bivalves are eaten by walruses, who rake them out of the mud with their tusks and swallow them whole. *A. castanea*, the chestnut astarte, is found along the northern Atlantic coast of the United States north to Nova Scotia. It is also found around the British Isles. This species is marked by a bright red foot. *A. undata* is found along the northern Atlantic and Pacific coasts of North America. Its brown shell has a number of strong ridges.

The Cardiacea. Members of the superfamily Cardiacea are commonly known as cockles, or heart shells. Their name stems from the fact that they look like a heart when viewed endwise. The many genera of this group are found all over the world.

The rounded shells of many species have numerous ribs and scalloped edges; some also have spines or scales. In others the valves have relatively smooth surfaces. The siphons are generally short. The foot is long and well-developed and may be used for leaping. There is no byssus, and the cockles live unattached. They range in size from about ½ inch to 6 inches.

The common, or edible, cockle, *Cerastodema edule*, is one of the most familiar bait and food bivalves in European coastal towns and city fish markets. Its shell bears about 25 bold ribs with nodules or scales if the creature lives in mud; these trimmings are worn off if it lives in sand. This mollusk is so adaptable to variations in the salinity of water that it can thrive equally well in highly saline lagoons and in the diluted waters of estuaries. It is the only mollusk that made its way into the Black Sea, and from there moved to the Azov Sea. More remarkable, it has even penetrated the salty Caspian Sea.

Species of the genera *Dinocardium*, *Laevicardium*, and *Trachycardium* are found along the coasts of North America. However, they are too tough to be edible. The shells of some species of cockles are highly prized by collectors.

The Tridacnacea. The superfamily Tridacnacea includes the giant clam, *Tridacna gigas*, the largest bivalve in the world. Anyone who has ever read adventure stories has undoubtedly come across at least one hair-raising tale of a diver who inadvertently steps between the shells of one of these giant creatures to be captured in a viselike grip until he drowns—unless rescue comes at the last possible moment.

The truth is that the giant clam could be a dangerous adversary. Measuring up to 4 feet in diameter and weighing up to 600 pounds, this monster is in a class by itself. The power exerted by its valves in closing is tremendous, and any creature caught in its grasp is very likely to be crushed. However, the valves close slowly and are filled by the fleshy mantle so that it is easy to escape being caught.

Surprisingly, the clam inside this immense shell weighs only 20 to 25 pounds. The meat has been described as good to eat. The great valves are often used as holy water fonts in Catholic churches. Natives of the Caroline Islands hew ax heads out of the thickest portions of the shell, which is remarkably hard. Until recently, natives of the Solomon Islands used sections of the hinge for barter.

Although it may be difficult to believe, giant clams may live for more than a century, existing immobile at shallow depths, tenaciously anchored by an extremely strong byssus. Their longevity can be attributed only to the fact that they have few successful natural enemies. Boring shells attack in great numbers, but rarely breach the massive shell to reach the animal inside.

Giant clams are commonly found among coral reefs in the Indo-Pacific region. The shell is generally white, sometimes tinged with red and saffron or yellow-brown. The

ally 4 to 8 inches long. These bivalves form extensive beds among the coral reefs and islands of the Indian and Pacific Oceans.

The bear's paw, *Hippopus hippopus,* is related to the giant clam. Members of this species, which occur throughout the western Pacific, are perhaps most plentiful in the Philippines, Melanesia, and Micronesia. The shell attains a length of over 12 inches; it is white with reddish-brown markings.

A piece of wood (left) has been cut away to show the shipworm Teredo navalis. *The animal secretes a chemical that disintegrates wood fibers. This enables the shipworm to work its way through the hardest woods.*

mantle is beautifully colored with iridescent shades of blue, violet, and yellow, and struck with fantastic markings. One early observer of these clams in Philippine waters wrote enthusiastically of passing over a mass of them, nearly a mile in extent—they "resembled nothing so much as a beautiful bed of tulips."

The genus *Tridacna* also includes smaller species, such as *T. squamosa,* which is usu-

The Mactracea. Members of the superfamily Mactracea are commonly known as surf clams. They are widely distributed and can be found even in the coldest seas. Surf clams are generally found in burrows along exposed shores. They generally have equal-sized valves that are rather triangular in shape. There are two long siphons that are fused together. The foot is strong and may be used for jumping.

Members of the genus *Mactra* have strong, thick shells and a large foot. This group includes about 150 species, which are found in all seas but are most abundant in the tropics.

Spisula solidissima is found along the Atlantic coast of North America from Labrador to the Carolinas. It is one of the larger bivalves in this range, with shells up to 7 inches in length. This clam is found in burrows in the sand in shallow waters.

Members of this species are sometimes used for food. They may be dug out with shovels or clam rakes by picnickers intent on a clambake. At high water, some fishermen still go after them with a sharp stick, which they poke into the bottom. The open valves of the clam will close at once if the stick should enter, and the fisherman can then pull his catch from the water.

Spisula falcata is a smaller species, measuring a little over 3 inches in length. It is found along the Pacific coasts of the United States and Mexico.

The Solenacea. Members of the superfamily Solenacea are called razor shells or razor clams. These very agile bivalves live buried vertically in the sand in a burrow a yard or more long. The shape of the shell—elongated valves that, when closed, give the shell the appearance of a tube or the handle of a barber's straight-edged razor—enables the animal to slip through sand or water with ease and speed.

When the razor clam is buried, two siphons extend from the forward end, just barely breaking the surface of the sand. At the opposite end of the shell is a well-developed foot that is relatively thin when the clam is digging, but which can swell up to serve as an anchor or contract to draw its owner down into the sand.

Ensis directus is a common razor clam found along the Atlantic coast from Labrador to southern Florida. The shell is about 6

inches long and yellow or green in color. This species of clams is edible.

Solen viridis is found from southern New England to Florida. It is only about 2 inches long, and its shell is green. *S. rosaceus* is also about 2 inches long. It is found along the coast of southern California. The delicate shell is pale pink.

Members of the genus *Siliqua* have smooth elliptical shells. *S. costata* is very common

in shallow waters from Nova Scotia to the middle-Atlantic states. It is about 2 inches long, and its fragile shell is green. *S. patula* also has a thin shell. It is about 5 inches long and is found from northern California to the Okhotsk Sea.

The Tellinacea. The superfamily Tellinacea is a large group, with more than 500 species found along the shores of all seas. Members of this group have equal-sized valves. There are two siphons. Most tellinids are white, but some are brilliantly colored. The most beautiful forms are found in the warm Pacific waters.

After heavy seas, beaches are often littered with thousands of fragile pink shells, lying with their valves open, looking like small butterflies. These are *Macoma tenuis*, common along Europe's Atlantic coast.

Macoma balthica is found in shallow waters on both the east and west coasts of North America north to the Arctic; it is also found along the coasts of Europe. The shell of this species is rounded and less than 1 inch in length. Individuals living on sandy habitats have thin shells that are white, pink,

or yellow; those living in mud have thick bluish or rusty-colored shells.

Other common genera in this group are *Tagelus* and *Tellina*, which include many of the highly colored tropical species.

Members of the family Donacidae are commonly known as wedge shells because of their triangular shape. In these mollusks the shell is thick and the foot is long. These bivalves may be found in brackish waters as well as in the ocean. They can be found in immense quantities on both coasts of the United States by following the receding tide. As the water exposes the sand, these strikingly colored little bivalves dive quickly out of sight, but can be sieved up by determined hunters.

The genus *Donax* contains about 100 species, several of which are found along the coasts of North America. *D. variabilis* is common in shallow water from Long Island to Texas. Its 1-inch shell is white.

The Arcticacea. The best-known representative of the superfamily Arcticacea is *Arctica islandica*. This bivalve is found in relatively deep waters from Long Island to the Arctic Ocean; it also inhabits the coasts of northern Europe. It once migrated to the Mediterranean during a colder period, but is now extinct there. In this species the dark shell is thick and wrinkled. It is about 3 inches in length.

The Glossacea. The superfamily Glossacea is closely related to the Arcticacea. The best known species of this group is *Glossus humanus*, or *Isocardia cor*, popularly known as the heart shell. It has a bulky shell that is unusual because of its reversed umboes. It is found in the Mediterranean down to considerable depths.

The Dreissenacea. Members of the superfamily Dreissenacea are similar to freshwater clams. The shells resemble those of the genus *Mytilus* except that there is no nacreous lining. *Dreissenia polymorpha* inhabits rivers, canals, and small creeks where the water is often slightly saline. A native of Asia, it has gradually penetrated Europe's lakes and streams. Hobbyists collect *Dreissenia* shells, which may vary considerably in form.

Another genus of this group is *Mytilopsis*. *M. leucophaetus* is found in fresh and brackish water in the southeastern United States. It lives attached by its byssus. The brown shell of this species is about ½ inch long.

The Corbiculacea. Members of the superfamily Corbiculacea are widespread in fresh

The fossil shell of a member of the superfamily Pleurotomariacea (left) was found in rocks of the Ordovician period. This means that it is more than 425 million years old. There are several hundred fossil species in this superfamily. A few living species have been found in the Caribbean and the Indo-Pacific marine provinces.

and brackish water. They are often very tiny, but *Corbicula fluminalis* attains a diameter of more than an inch. Commonly found in the rice fields of Asia, members of this species have a shiny, ridged, dark green shell with darker patches.

The Veneracea. The superfamily Veneracea contains several hundred species that are found in all seas. Many of the tropical species have elegant shapes, coloring, and markings. The shells of this group are thick and heavy. The hinge has an interlocking system of three cardinal teeth in each valve. Free-moving, active animals, they rarely burrow or tie themselves down with a byssus.

Mercenaria mercenaria is the chief commercial clam of the Atlantic coast. It goes by several popular names—quahog, little neck, hardshell, and round clam. To this list should be added cherrystone clams, since they are only smaller, immature specimens of the same species. These clams are particularly popular during the summer, when oysters are not available. In this species the inside of the oval shell is a porcelaneous white, with violet splashes near the muscle scars and a violet border around the ventral margin. The hard-shell clam reaches 4 inches in length and 2½ inches in width. It ranges from Nova Scotia to the West Indies and into the Gulf of Mexico.

The closely related species, *Mercenaria campechiensis*, occurs from Virginia to Texas. This is a large bivalve, with a diameter of 6 inches and a weight sometimes reaching 5 pounds. Its flesh is coarser in texture and stronger in flavor than the northern species, but southerners in coastal areas catch them in quantities and turn them into a passable chowder.

Callanaitis disjecta, common in Australia and Tasmania, is one of the most beautiful of the venerids, or Venus clams. It has curved pink fronds and a delicate structure. *Gemma gemma*, the amethystine gem shell, is

smaller than a pea but is truly a jewel of a shell. Its shining surface is closely crowded with concentric furrows, and it ranges from white or rose at one end to reddish-purple at the other. This species is common in sand and shallow waters on the east and west coasts of North America.

The Myacea. The superfamily Myacea includes the soft-shell clams of northern waters. The best-known members are probably *Mya arenaria*, the long-neck, or soft-shell, clam, and *Mya truncata*, the short clam. Both have roughly the same characteristics, but the long-neck clam has been better known ever since the Indians introduced it to the Pilgrims.

The Indian name *maninose* was corrupted to nannynose by the white man, and is still heard along the Eastern seaboard. In En-

glish markets, shoppers ask for sand gapers or old maids when they want soft-shell clams. These are important food clams, but they are inferior to the hard-shell clam in taste.

Soft-shells burrow in the sand between low- and high-tide marks. People who walk the beach can tell by the little spurts of water

The abalone Haliotis cracherodi, *found along the western coast of the United States, has a black exterior with shadings of purple and green. About eight of the holes on its shell are open. Its only sculpturing consists of growth lines.*

rising from the wet sand that the animal underneath has suddenly drawn its siphon down as a measure of safety. This action apparently does not disturb the little snail *Odostomia trifida*, which occupies a curious habitat on the end of the siphon of the soft-shell clam.

In the genus *Corbula* the shells are small and thick, and the valves are not equal in size. *C. luteola,* found along the California coast, is yellow in color with some purple marks. It is about ½ inch in length. *C. contracta* lives along the east coast from New England to Florida. It is about ½ inch long and its shell is marked with concentric ridges.

The Hiatellacea. The superfamily Hiatellacea includes *Panopea generosa*, the largest bivalve on the west coast of North America.

The average length is 6 inches, but larger specimens are common. The siphons on this species are big—a yard in length and thicker than a stout broom handle. Thick, wrinkled skin protects the siphon, giving it the appearance of a small elephant trunk. This tube accounts for more than half the weight of the animal, which can be as much as 16 pounds.

Indians in the Puget Sound area called this whopper of a clam gweduck, and the name has been corrupted to gooeyduck. The animal is so big it bulges out of its shell, and the siphon still sticks out a foot or more even when fully retracted. Indeed, this clam is so large and difficult to handle that it is a rare hunter who can capture one by himself. The effort is worthwhile, however, for those who have feasted on the gooeyduck describe it as delicious.

Slender tentacles extend from holes in the shell of the abalone Haliotis lamellosa, *known in Europe as the sea ear. The inside of the shell is lined with a beautiful, iridescent mother-of-pearl. The meat is considered a delicacy.*

The Pholadacea. In the superfamily Pholadacea, a group of extremely capable wood and rock borers, the teredo, or shipworm, *Teredo navalis*, is probably the best known —and certainly the most hated—species. When wooden ships sailed the seas, the shipworm was a worse scourge than any pirate. Even today crumbled piers and jetties can be blamed to a large extent on this insidious destroyer.

The shells of the shipworm are only about ½ inch long, while the body, at maturity, reaches a length of 6 to 12 inches in northern waters and 2 feet in the tropics. This animal hatches in the spring and starts life as a free-swimming larva. In a week or two, grown to the size of a pinhead, it bores a hole into submerged wood just big enough for its body. This hole on the outer surface of the wood never gets any larger, but the tunnel connected to it inside the wood is made larger as the worm increases in size. In effect, the shipworm is a prisoner of its own making; it must stay in its wooden jail, burrowing this way and that, until the wood crumbles. The minuteness of the initial hole it bores accounts for the fact that a ship bottom or piling can appear perfectly sound until it collapses.

One kind word can be said about this marine pest: given time, it will also clear harbors and waterways of wrecked hulks, driftwood, submerged stumps, and any other wooden debris that constitutes a menace to navigation.

The rock-boring Pholadacea include the wing shells and some piddocks. They drill and enlarge their burrows, sometimes as deep as a foot, by constantly turning their abrasive shells around and around. The hypothesis that boring is assisted by acid secretions has not been substantiated. Most biologists now believe that the shell, although fragile and delicate, is rendered into an abrasive rasping tool by the hard ridges on it.

A curious fact is that the holes of these animals never intersect with each other, even though their colonies are always densely populated.

The larger species of this group, such as angel wings and most piddocks, live in burrows in soft mud or clay.

The Anomalodesmata

The subclass Anomalodesmata is composed mostly of burrowing bivalves. A number of specialized groups are included— spoon shells and duck shells, for example— and some of them appear to be survivors of very ancient groups. Their valves are usually unequal, their shells are generally thin, and the hinge is poorly developed and without a hinge plate. They range in size from medium to small, and they are hermaphroditic.

The Pandoracea. The superfamily Pandoracea contains bivalves whose valves are commonly unequal in size. The members of this group are varied in their life style. Some are free living, some become attached to the substratum, others burrow in the sand, and still others live in mucus tubes.

Pandora inaequivalvis is a common mollusk of the Mediterranean and the Atlantic coast of Europe. *P. gouldiana,* a delicate little shell, pearly white and oval, ranges from Prince Edward Island to New Jersey. *P. trilineata* is common in shallow water

The common European limpet, Patella vulgata *(below left), belongs to the family of Old World limpets. Their conical shells, solid and strongly ribbed, form a peak that is tipped slightly to the side. A widespread species, they can be found from the Arctic to the Mediterranean.*

Limpets can move short distances, but they always return to the same spot on a rock. They remain there for such long periods that the sharp edge of the shell carves an imprint into the hard stone (below right).

from North Carolina to Texas. It is less than 1½ inches in length.

In the genus *Thracia* the shell may grow to considerable size. The valves are nearly equal, and the umbos are prominent. The giant thracia, *T. conradi,* is the largest species of the genus, sometimes rivaling the soft clam in dimensions. The shell is ashy white, thin, and fragile. The siphons are quite long. Ranging from Labrador to New York, it is especially abundant off New England. This species lives buried in sandy or muddy bottoms in shallow water.

The Clavagellacea. Members of the superfamily Clavagellacea produce a calcareous tube in which their minute shells are embedded. In genera such as *Clavagella* the tube is attached to one valve only; in others, such as *Penicillus,* it is attached to both. In this latter genus, the tube is trumpet-shaped and bears several large ruffles toward the larger end.

The watering-pot shell, *Penicillus australis,* is small, but its mantle secretes a trumpet tube reaching 7 inches in length. Two insignificant valves are imbedded near the base of the tube. This strange creature has far outgrown its shell and altered the organs of its body to suit a new circumstance. It is found from the Red Sea to Australia.

The Poromyacea. Members of the family Cuspidariidae of the superfamily Poromyacea have beautiful small shells, elegantly ornate and curving to a beak at the end. There are about 20 species on the Atlantic coast, found mostly in deep water.

Cuspidaria pellucida is a small bivalve found from New England northward. Its smooth, white shell is less than ½ inch long. *C. pectinata* is found along the Pacific coast of the United States, Mexico, and Central America. Its shell is characterized by 12 radiating ribs. It is only about ⅕ inch long.

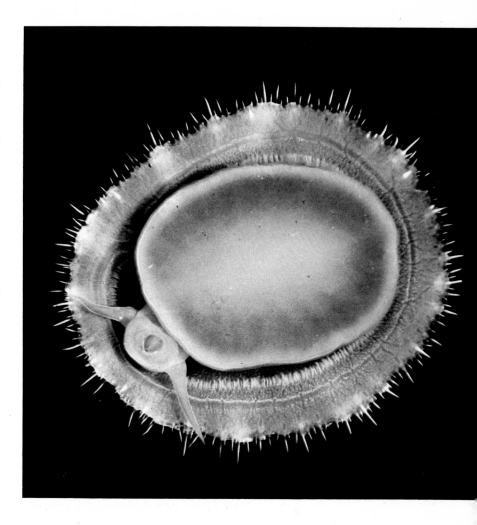

Snails— Gastropoda

The Gastropoda, the snails, are the largest class of mollusks. They are also the most successful class in terms of evolution. Including more than 75,000 species, they are found on land, in fresh water, and in the seas. They are diverse in their feeding habits and include herbivores, carnivores, and parasites, as well as scavengers and filter feeders. Most of these animals have only one shell—they are sometimes called univalves—which is usually in the form of a spiral. Snails are

The limpet Patella lusitanica *(above) is found in the Mediterranean. This photo, taken from underneath the animal, shows the well-developed foot and the tentacles that extend from the head.*

characterized by a twisted, one-sided anatomy and a broad, flat foot. Gastropods have recognizable heads; there are usually two eyes, one on each side of the head. There are also well-developed organs of smell on tentacles projecting from the head.

Some species of snails are eaten, particularly by the French, and they are considered a great delicacy.

Anatomy

In spite of the diversity found in this large class, the gastropods do have many common characteristics.

The Shell. The shells of gastropods vary greatly in size, shape, and color. There is also a wide variety of ornamentation. Most

The marine snail Calliostoma granulatum is shown here fully expanded against the glass wall of an aquarium. Usually about an inch high, this snail has threadlike ribs set with fine beading, which give its surface a granular appearance.

are in the form of a cone-shaped spiral, which is wound around a central column called the *columella*. The turns of the spiral are called *whorls*. The smallest whorl, at the apex of the shell, is the oldest. The largest whorl, the body whorl, ends in an opening, or aperture, from which the head and foot of the snail protrude. The turns of the spiral can be either clockwise or counterclockwise, although in most it is clockwise. Generally, the whorls are in contact, with a suture line between adjacent turns.

Gastropod shells consist of three layers. The thin outer layer, called the *periostracum*, is composed of a horny substance called conchiolin. The two inner layers consist of calcium carbonate. In the middle *prismatic layer* this compound is in the form of vertical crystals, while in the inner *nacreous layer* it is present in thin sheets.

The foot and head of most snails can be withdrawn into the shell by a retractor muscle. In many species there is a horny disc in the foot that blocks the opening when the animal is inside the shell. This protective disc is called the *operculum*.

The Foot. The foot, which is on the ventral side of the body, may be long and well-developed or rudimentary, depending on the species. It is the only means of locomotion in snails, and is well-adapted for use on a variety of surfaces—rocks; soft, muddy, or sandy bottoms; and terrestrial vegetation. There is a pedal gland that opens on the foot and secretes a trail of slimy mucus; the mucus holds the foot to the substratum. In most forms locomotion is brought about by continuous waves of contraction that pass from one end of the foot to the other.

In groups of marine snails that lead a pelagic existence, the foot has become modified for swimming. In sessile snails, on the other hand, the foot is modified for attachment to the substratum.

Internal Anatomy. Like the spiral shells, the internal organs also undergo a twisting, or torsion. As previously mentioned, the head and foot can protrude through the aperture of the shell, but the visceral mass always remains within the large whorls.

The twisting of both the body and the shell is foreshadowed in the segmentation

The snail Cochlostoma septemspirale *(above left) has a shell with seven spirals. This European species is a land-dwelling member of the super-family Cyclophoracea. It is often found in woodlands under damp stones and rotting leaves.*

The sea snail Monodonta lineata *(above right) lives along the Atlantic coast of Europe. These snails spend many hours out of water. They often gather in rock crevices just above the water line.*

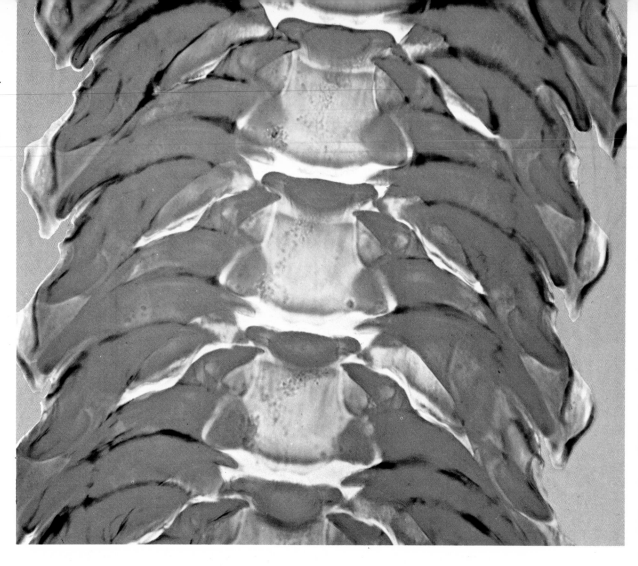

This photo is an enlargement of the radula, or tongue covering, of the periwinkle Littorina littorea. *The surface of the radula is composed of lines of teeth. Each line includes a central tooth and two pairs of side teeth.*

of the egg and begins during the free-swimming larval period. In their earliest phase the larvae of gastropods exhibit a bilateral symmetry; the original mantle and shell are cap-shaped, the intestine is straight, and the mouth and anus are at opposite ends of the body with the developing foot between them. But then the front edge of the conical shell, together with the body and organs of the animal, twist 180 degrees to the right. As a result, the body makes a half turn and the anal opening is brought up front near the mouth; the other organs normally found at the rear also move around to establish themselves near the head.

This torsion also causes a rotation of the nervous system, which results in a crossover of nerve cords; gastropods of this type are called the Streptoneura. In other forms the initial torsion is followed by a countertorsion that modifies some of the organs and eliminates the crossover of nerve cords; these gastropods are called the Euthyneura.

As the shell twists with the growth of the snail, each spiral is reflected in a turning of the visceral mass of the animal within. The organs on the outside of the spiral grow unretarded, while those on the inside become compressed. This affects the paired structures, such as the ctenidia, or gills, the kidneys, and the auricles of the heart; one of each pair degenerates and disappears while the other develops fully. In this way a symmetrical animal becomes asymmetrical.

The mantle lines the body whorl. The space between the mantle and the parts of the body that can be protruded from the shell is the mantle cavity. Sometimes the edge of the mantle curves back into itself, forming a siphon that functions in respiration.

The digestive tract begins with a muscular pharynx with a pair of jaws. One or two pairs of salivary glands open into the pharynx. There is a long esophagus followed by a stomach, a winding intestine, and a hindgut, or rectum. Ducts lead from the stomach to a large liver, or *midgut gland.*

Except in parasitic forms, the floor of the pharynx usually contains a radula. This well-developed organ is covered with teeth, which number from less than twenty to several thousand. These teeth are always arranged in rows. Since the shape and arrangement of the teeth is quite constant within groups, they are important in the classification of gastropods.

Most aquatic snails breathe through gills consisting of a comb of fringed respiratory plates. The location of the gills depends on the amount of torsion undergone in the development of the animal. In the Prosobranchia, in which the torsion is complete, the gills are situated in front of the heart. In the Ophisthobranchia the gills are behind the heart. In others, the respiratory exchange takes place through the general body surface. In terrestrial snails there is a lung instead of gills.

The heart of the gastropod, located on the dorsal side, has one ventricle and one or two auricles. The number of auricles possessed by an individual depends on whether that animal has one or two gills.

In most snails the sexes are separate, with a single, unpaired gonad. In hermaphroditic forms there is a single hermaphroditic gonad. Unlike the bivalves, fertilization in the gastropods is generally internal. The copulating organ is usually located in the forward part of the body to the right. Even among the hermaphrodites, copulation is more customary between individuals than is self-fertilization.

Periwinkles of the species Littorina neritoides *(below left) are attached by dry mucus to sun-baked rocks. This animal can survive out of water for as long as five months.*

Three specimens of the periwinkle Littorina obtusata *(below) have bright yellow shells. This is the normal color of the species, but there are many variations in shading and pattern.*

Classification

The classification followed here is based on the division of the Gastropoda into three subclasses: Prosobranchia, Opisthobranchia, and Pulmonata.

The Prosobranchia. This subclass includes a large number of mollusks that are predominantly marine and are almost always provided with a shell. This adornment is usually twisted into a spiral, but on occasion it can be shaped like a tube, cup, or pan. The sexes are separate in most of these snails. The form of the radula varies a great deal from one group to another, and therefore is particularly helpful in identification.

The Opisthobranchia. In the Opisthobranchia, the gills are generally situated to the rear, hence the name (*opistho* meaning "hind," *branchia* meaning "gill"). In some families the shell is well developed and external; in others it is thin and covered by the mantle; and in still others it is completely lacking. These marine snails are hermaphroditic.

The Pulmonata. The subclass Pulmonata includes terrestrial and freshwater snails, with a few marine species. These gastropods have lungs rather than gills. They have shells, usually of the typical spiral form, but no operculum. Pulmonates vary rather widely in size. All members of this subclass are hermaphroditic—that is, they produce both egg and sperm cells.

Gastropods of the Past

The earliest snails known belonged to the Prosobranchia and date from the Lower Cambrian period, 600 to 550 million years ago. The Pulmonata evolved during the Devonian period, 410 to 350 million years ago. About 350 to 275 million years ago, during the Carboniferous period, the first

Shore periwinkles, Littorina littorea, are a popular delicacy in France despite their small size. They are marketed under such names as Bigorneau, Vigneau, and Brelin. The species has spread from the coast of northern Europe to the North American Atlantic coast.

representatives of the Opisthobranchia appeared.

The early Prosobranchia belonged to the Archaeoteropoda, a group that still boasts living representatives in such genera as *Patella* and *Nerita*. A number of other genera died out, however. Among them were the widely distributed *Bellerophon*, which lived from the Silurian period to the Triassic period; *Pterotheca*, an inhabitant of both North America and Europe; and the elegantly ornate *Tremonotus*.

The Helcionellacea, distributed through Asia, Africa, Europe, and North America, included a few species that dated from the earliest Cambrian years and became extinct just before the very end of the Cambrian period.

Enormous accumulations of land-snail shells from the Quarternary period are common, particularly in caves and natural cavities, where underground waters washed them into huge heaps and cemented them together in calcareous deposits. Numerous pulmonate fossils—including those in the genera *Helix Bulimus*, and *Clausilia*—have also been found in ancient coastal dunes excavated by researchers.

The most drastic change in the evolution of the gastropods from the hypothetical common ancestor of the mollusks was the twisting, or torsion, of the internal organs. This was different from the spiraling of the shell, which evolved before torsion. From fossil evidence, it is known that the earliest spiral shells were not conical but flat and disc-shaped, like a coiled hose. The torsion of the soft parts of the body occurred later. The development of the typically cone-shaped spiral shell of the gastropods was the last great evolutionary change.

In the following sections some of the representative members of each superfamily will be discussed.

The Archaeogastropoda

Members of the order Archaeogastropoda are often described as the most primitive living prosobranchs. These animals usually have two gills, two auricles, and two kidneys. In some, however, one of the pair of these organs may be reduced or even lacking. The fact that these organs are present in pairs is considered to be a primitive condition. Although mostly marine, some members of this order are found in fresh or brackish water. The shell of these mollusks is either spiral or cup-like.

The Pleurotomariacea. The Pleurotomariacea is a mostly extinct superfamily. Its living members are characterized by the presence of a long, deep notch in the shell, corresponding to a recess in the mantle where the anal outlet is located. The family Pleurotomariidae is the most primitive of this primitive group.

The photographic enlargements (below) of hydrobiid snail shells collected from springs and water supply systems in northern Italy include:
A. Bythinella schmidti
B. Frauenfeldia lacheineri
C. *a member of the genus Avenionia*
D. *a member of the genus Pseudamnicola*
E. Lartetia virei
F. Lartetia concii
G. Paladilhia vobarnensis
H. Iglica percoi
I. Pseudamnicola insubrica
L. *a member of the genus Hauffenia*
M. Sadleriana fluminensis

They reached their maximum development during the Paleozoic and Mesozoic eras, and are now in the process of becoming extinct. There are only about a dozen living species, all of them rare. They are found at great depths in the seas around the West Indies, southeast Africa, Japan, and the southwest Pacific.

Their shells are very beautiful and much in demand for collections. At the turn of the century, a fine 5-inch specimen of *Entemnotrochus adansoniana,* taken alive from a 100-fathom depth off Guadaloupe, was priced at £100 sterling in London.

The family Haliotidae includes the abalones. In this group the last turn of the spiral is so large it constitutes practically the whole of the shell. The shell is also spectacularly iridescent, and for years it has been in great demand for use in button and ornament manufacture and mother-of-pearl inlays.

In these creatures the notch is replaced by a series of holes; through most of these holes extend feelers from the mantle. The hindermost hole serves as the anal opening. The outer layer of the shell is unicolored in most species but may be variegated or multicolored, particularly in many of the smaller species. When this layer is removed, the outside of the shell is also pearly.

Most species of Haliotidae inhabit the waters of the Pacific and Indian oceans. The large foot is so powerful that it is almost impossible to pry the animal loose from the rock it is grasping unless it is taken by surprise. The meat of the foot makes delicious "steak" and is popular in California. Consumption there is miniscule, however, compared to the demand in the Far East, especially in China and Japan, where it is a staple diet item and is considered a symbol of long life and prosperity.

The members of the Scissurellidae are so small that they usually escape notice. Seen through a magnifying glass, however, their tiny shells show beautiful ornamentation.

The Fissurellacea. The superfamily Fissurellacea includes only one family, the Fissurellidae, the keyhole limpets. In this group the shell is broadly conical, with a tentlike spire. They differ from other limpets in having an opening, or keyhole, usually located in the apex. In the subfamily Emarginulinae the opening may be at the apex, at the margin of the shell, or lacking. Generally small, keyhole limpets live on submerged stones and feed on algae and waste vegetable matter.

The Patellacea. Members of the superfamily Patellacea are commonly known as limpets. These primitive mollusks have a conical, nonspiraling shell.

Of the Patellacea, species of the families Patellidae and Acmaeidae are considered edible. They are generally swallowed raw, but it has been noticed that the extremely long radula, especially in the case of the large species, can cause some painful gastric disturbances in humans.

Perhaps the most remarkable thing about the limpet is its extremely strong foot. The poet Wordsworth paid tribute to that sturdy member with this rhyme: "Should the strongest arm endeavour/The limpet from its rock

The turreted form of two unrelated families of marine snails can be noted in the shells of Cerithium vulgata *(upper) of the family* Cerithidae *and that of* Turritella triplicata *(lower) of the family* Turritellidae. *It was believed to have been a shell of the latter group that gave the Greek philosopher Archimedes the inspiration for the Archimedean screw.*

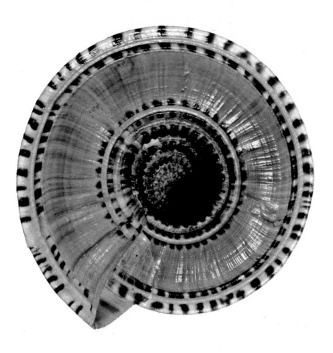

to sever /'Tis seen its loved support to clasp/ With such tenacity to grasp/We wonder that such strength should dwell/In such a small and simple shell."

The family Patellidae, the Old World limpets, are found in large numbers along rocky reefs in all seas. A total of about 400 species are known. The lining of their shells is smoothed out to fit their shells. The strong times almost translucent. The surface of the shell is generally striated.

These limpets choose a spot on a rocky surface and there sink a shallow pit, which is smoothed out to fit their shells. The strong foot enables them to cling tenaciously, and considerable power is required to move them; they resist quite successfully the buffeting of very large waves. They can leave their selected place for short explorations, ranging over the rocks to feed on the minute vegetation that grows here and there in patches, but they always return to the same place. The radulas of many limpets scraping the surface of the rock as they feed make a peculiar noise. At rest, the radula is coiled like a watch spring.

Unlike their near relatives, the limpets of this family have gills that are reduced to mere stumps; instead there is a series of gill plates encircling the mantle. With this breathing apparatus the animal can remain out of seawater for hours, and can withstand exposure to sun or rain without inconvenience.

Patellidae are widely distributed in the eastern and southern hemispheres. The common tent shell, *Patella vulgata*, ranges from arctic shores southward to Spain. The rusty limpet, *P. ferruginea*, is very heavy and deeply sculptured with ridges radiating from the apex. The back of the shell is rust-brown, shaded with wavy lines of white. The lining is white and like porcelain. Its habitat is the Mediterranean.

The tropical regions hold the finest specimens of these tentlike shells. *P. longicosta*, from South Africa, has ridges on its heavy shell that extend into thin bladelike projections. *P. granularis* has a peaked roof studded with stout spikes. The shell of *Patella aspersa* of Madeira has a set of saw-toothed ridges as sharp as knife blades.

Patella compressa is so-named because its thin shell is compressed at the sides to conform to the shape of its host, *Ecklonia*, the sea bamboo.

P. mexicana is the giant of the family. Its shell is ponderous and bowl-shaped. It ranges in length from 6 to 14 inches, and with its hard white porcelainlike lining, it is reputed to have been used as a wash basin in Central America.

Helcion pectinata from South Africa is typical of the cap-shaped limpets. The apex of its shell points forward while the slope behind it is decidedly curved. Limpets of this shape are sometimes known as clowns' caps. This animal's ribs are black and prickly, with buff or pink grooves in between.

Other genera of the family Patellidae are *Nacella* and *Cellana*. *Cellana radians* from New Zealand has a shell with a finely mot-

The tropical snail Architectonia perspectiva *has one of the most beautiful of snail shells (left). The shell is usually 1 to 2 inches across. This gastropod, commonly called the sundial, is found in the Indo-Pacific provinces. A similar form occurs in the West Indies.*

The gracefully turreted snail shell (below left) belongs to Epitonium clathrus, *which is found along the coasts of the Atlantic and the Mediterranean. These animals are commonly known as wentletraps, or staircase shells, wentletrap is a Dutch word that means "spiral staircase."*

The violet snail Janthina janthina *(below center) is a sea mollusk that floats upside down just below the surface of the water. It floats with the aid of a bubble-filled raft of mucus that it secretes from its foot. These sightless creatures feed on much larger jellyfish. If attacked, violet snails exude a cloud of purple "ink."*

tled exterior and a lining that looks like smoked pearl. The lining may also be a metallic gold.

The members of the family Acmaeidae have a conical shell similar to that of the Old World limpets, but it is smaller in size and the lining is more porcelaneous than iridescent. The apex is almost always at the center or displaced forward, and the embryonic portion of the shell is conical rather than spiral, as in the Patellidae.

The tortoise shell limpet, *Acmaea testudinalis*, has a wide distribution. In the Western Hemisphere it inhabits the New England coast and is found north to Labrador; it reaches a length of 1½ inches. In the British

Isles it is smaller. In a roughly tesselated pattern, brown and green stripes radiate from the apex, crossing concentric circles of white and black on a gray background. A variant of this species, *Acmaea testudinalis alvea*, extends the range to the Arctic Ocean. It has compressed sides, and is about the same width as the blades of the eelgrass on which it lives.

The plate limpet, *Acmaea scutum*, is closely related to the tortoise shell limpet of the Atlantic. Found along the Pacific coast of North America, this limpet is about 2 inches long.

The following species are also found on the west coast of North America. The rough

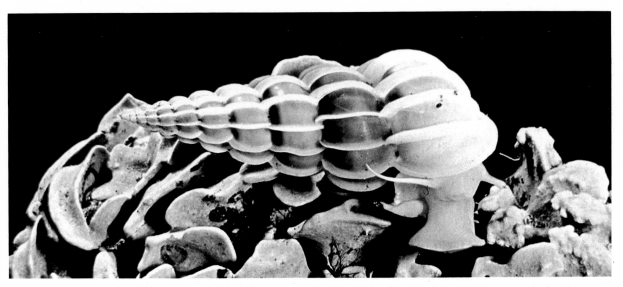

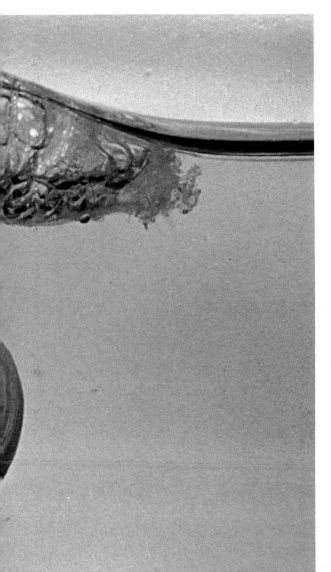

limpet, *Acmaea digitalis*, has scaly ridges and black flesh. The ghost limpet, *Acmaea scabra*, has an impression reminiscent of a human hand showing under the white callus lining its shell.

Lottia gigantica, the only species of this genus, is found from northern California to Mexico. About 3½ inches long, its shell is dark brown.

The third family of the Patellacea, the Lepetidae, has only a few representatives, most of them denizens of the colder seas. Members of this group do not have eyes or gills.

The Cocculinacea. The superfamily Cocculinacea includes only a few creatures, all of whom have cuplike shells. The species of this group form part of the fauna of the ocean abysses. They have no eyes, and there is usually only one gill.

The Trochacea. Many members of the superfamily Trochacea are commonly called top shells because the shell is formed into a top-shaped conical spire. Unlike the Patel-

lacea, the Trochacea can withdraw into their shells. In most there is an operculum to cover over the opening.

The largest family of this group, the Trochidae, contains over fifty genera with more than a thousand species. These animals are usually found at shallow depths clinging to the rocks and reefs. Some species are also found in crevices in the rocks above the waterline, positions in which they can exist for a considerable period of time with only the spray from breakers providing them with necessary moisture. They feed on nearby vegetation.

A snail of this type is the common *Monodonta turbinata,* a species with a strong, rounded shell and a horny operculum that fits perfectly in the shell opening. The surface of the shell is marbled and marked by fine lines of white, brown, and green, which give it excellent protective coloring amid rocks.

The top shells are chiefly tropical, with only a comparative handful of the many species common in waters around North America. Some of these are included in the genus *Margarites,* and most of them are very small. *M. olivacea,* olive brown in color and only ¼ inch in diameter, ranges from Labrador to Massachusetts. The wavy top shell, *Margarites groenlandicus,* is ⅓ inch in diameter, but its pearly iridescence makes a shining display when a number of individuals are gathered in a rock crevice at low tide.

Species common in warmer European waters include *Gibbula richardi,* a snail easily recognized by its smooth, depressed shell and large white umbilicus—in certain gastropods, a hollow forming the middle point around which the shell is twisted. The outer surface of this shell is often corroded, allowing the magnificently iridescent mother-of-pearl underlining to shine through.

Members of the family Turbinidae have a calcareous rather than horny operculum.

An air bubble is about to escape from the mucus float of the snail Janthina janthina (left). Snails of this species swim through the water supported only by their bubble raft.

The shell is large, spiral, and turban-shaped, with a rounded opening and an interior lined with mother-of-pearl. The outer surface is often ornamented. Some of the warm-water species are especially in demand for their vivid coloring and beautiful nacreous lining.

The turban shells of the genus *Turbo* include the green snail, *T. marmoratus,* which is found in the Indian Ocean. It is 4 to 8 inches long; its highly ornamental shell is bright green.

The Neritacea. The superfamily Neritacea contains three families, which show a gradual transition from the primitive marine forms to the more highly evolved terrestrial forms. The first family, the Neritopsidae, consists of extinct marine snails, except for one living species, *Neritopsis radula.* In this species the shell still displays the internal divisions that have been reabsorbed in other families.

The family Neritidae includes hundreds of species. These animals prefer coastal areas of temperate to tropical warmth; they are found in fresh running water as well as brackish and salt water.

The bleeding tooth, *Nerita peleronta,* is well known among coastal dwellers in Florida. The inner lip of the shell bears two teeth, either or both of which are stained with an orange "bloody" patch. *Nerita* shells

The magnificent precious wentletrap, Epitonium scalare *(opposite page), has been esteemed for several hundred years. Once considered valuable, the shells later were found in abundance off the east coast of Australia, causing a sharp drop in the market. Before that, specimens had been obtained in China. That Chinese craftsmen were supposed to have made rice paste counterfeits is a tale that has been told repeatedly.*

are generally solid and sometimes extraordinarily thick; they are round and smooth or grooved, with the opening often fantastically toothed.

A similar genus, *Neritina,* is almost as numerous as *Nerita* but the shell is usually much thinner. Some species are ornamented with spines, and one species found in the Philippines, *N. communis,* exhibits the greatest variation of brilliant coloration found in marine snails. In species from other areas the shells are all black or marked with a variety of dark shades.

A third genus, *Navicella,* comes mostly from the Pacific area. Members of this genus differ in shape from the preceding two genera, being more limpetlike. But like *Neritina* they are fond of locations in or near saltwater marshes.

The marine genus *Puperita* is known for its bizarre shells; *Puperita pupa,* for example, has a zebra-striped pattern. *Smaragdia viridis* is characterized by its pea-green color. *Theodoxus fluviatilis* is a common freshwater species in northern regions, and is found in rivers, streams, and canals throughout Europe.

The third family of this group, the Helicinidae, includes about 30 terrestrial genera that are distributed around the world except for the arctic region, where only fossil forms are found. They are small-to-medium sized snails that are most abundant in Central America and the islands of the Caribbean.

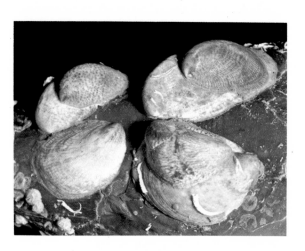

The Mesogastropoda

Mesogastropoda is a vast order with numerous superfamilies. All species are provided with shells, all have a heart with only one auricle, and there is only one kidney. The sexes are almost always separate. The shell assumes many different shapes, but usually forms a spiral.

The Cyclophoracea. The superfamily Cyclophoracea includes a large number of terrestrial and freshwater snails that are common in practically all parts of the world. The shell is usually conical and depressed. In this group respiration is accomplished by a specialized part of the mantle wall that acts as a lung.

The family Cyclophoridae includes about 70 genera, which are most common in the

Arched slipper shells of the species Crepidula fornicata *(right) are found along the east coast of North America, from Nova Scotia to the Gulf of Mexico. These boat-shaped limpets begin life as males and end it as females. In between, the animal passes through a stage in which it has both male and female reproductive organs.*

Hungarian cap-shells of the species Capulus hungaricus *(below) have a large, turned-down peak on their shell. These members of the family Calyptraeacea sometimes live as parasites of sea cucumbers.*

warmer parts of the world. The genus *Cyclophorus*, found in Southeast Asia, China, Japan, and the Philippines, contains many species that are noted for the size of their shells. *C. urantiacus*, for example, a snail found in Indonesia, reaches more than 2 inches in diameter.

In northern latitudes, genera of both the terrestrial and freshwater types abound. A familiar one is *Cochlostoma*, whose representatives are frequently found among damp rocks and under rotting leaves.

Members of the family Viviparidae are found in northern areas, including North America. Females of this family brood their young in the uterus. Two common genera of this group are *Viviparus* and *Campeloma*.

The largest living specimens of freshwater snails are members of the family Ampullariidae, which are found in tropical and subtropical areas. *Ampullarius urceus* has a spherical shell 4 inches or more in diameter.

Members of this genus are commonly kept in freshwater aquaria.

The Valvatacea. The living members of the superfamily Valvatacea are limited to one genus of the family Valvatidae. Species of the genus *Valvata* are found in the northern hemisphere, where they favor the muddy bottoms of freshwater lakes and streams. Most representatives of the superfamily, however, are found exclusively in fossil forms. *Valvata piscinalis* has a spherical shell with a circular lip. *Valvata cristata* is very small and has lungs as well as gills.

The Littorinacea. The superfamily Littorinacea includes periwinkles, chink shells, and others. They are mostly small or moderate-sized gastropods with conical shells. Although marine mollusks, they are not fond of being submerged. They crowd in groups among rocks between the tide levels, and

An immature specimen of the pink conch, Strombus gigas *(left), has emerged partially from its shell. The snail's eye is visible on the end of a fleshy stalk. Its foot is thrust into the sand, as the animal tries to right itself.*

often in areas reached only by the highest tides. They can survive long periods without water; indeed, if a number of them are placed in an aquarium containing a stone that juts out of the water, they will soon all be found on the dry part of the stone.

The family Littorinidae, in addition to marine forms, contains some species that live in fresh water, some in brackish water, and even some that live on the aerial roots of mangrove trees, hanging over the water and awaiting periodic dashes of spray.

The periwinkles are members of the genus *Littorina*. In these animals the shell is a conical spire of a few whorls; it has a round opening but lacks both umbilicus and pearly lining. The animal has a short, broad snout, and there are eyes on the outer sides of its long tentacles. The foot, broad and square, is divided into two parts, right and left; the parts work alternately, like human feet, as the animal inches slowly forward. The radula is narrow and long—about 2½ inches, or three times as long as the body. It is equipped with several hundred rows of sharp teeth for scraping algae off rocks. Owners of oyster beds, knowing the voracious appetite of vegetarian periwinkles, sometimes sprinkle these mollusks around their oyster beds to keep encroaching algae down to reasonable levels.

The name periwinkle is an old one. Apparently it has been modified from the phrase "petty winkle," used in London markets years ago to distinguish between this small animal and the large winkle, or whelk. Both creatures have long been staple foods in England and in other European countries. Women and children once made their livelihood by collecting thousands of these dingy little mollusks from the rocky coasts of the British Isles and selling them from corner stalls or pushcarts in the larger towns.

The shore, or edible, periwinkle, *Littorina littorea*, is an immigrant from Europe to the Atlantic shores of North America, having arrived via Iceland and Newfoundland. In its southward spread, it is meeting the lined periwinkle, *L. irrorata*, which occurs from the Gulf states northward to New Jersey.

The shell of the shore periwinkle is a thick, squat cone with seven or eight whorls and a sharp spire. It is yellowish-brown, olive, gray, or sometimes black. Often it is banded with brown or dark red. The length and height are each about 1 inch; males are smaller than females.

The lined periwinkle is the same size—about 1 inch. It can be recognized by its yellow-white color speckled with numerous

chestnut-brown spots in spiral rows on the whorls. The inner lip is brown, or sometimes orange.

The rough winkle, *L. saxatilis*, can be found on both the Atlantic and Pacific coasts. It is at most scarcely ½ inch in length, and is gray with inconspicuous bands of yellow, brown, or black. It can live out of water for at least a week. The checkered periwinkle, *L. scutulata*, and the eroded periwinkle, *L. planaxis*, are two similar West Coast species—about ½ inch in diameter. Found from Puget Sound south, their shells

The free-swimming gastropod Carinaria lamarcki *(right) is thin, transparent, and graceful. Its delicate shell is also very thin, fragile, and transparent. Because it lives in the open ocean, it is very seldom seen or collected.*

have black, brown, yellow, or green checks. The bizarrely striped zigzag periwinkle, *L. ziczac,* ranges from Florida to the West Indies.

The family Lacunidae, the chink shells, are conical, thin-shelled mollusks with a large opening shaped like a half moon. A long groove, or chink, in the inner lip leads to an umbilicus. The lip is sharp. The operculum is a thin, spiral membrane.

The Atlantic chink shell, *Lacuna vincta,* looks at first glance like a long, thin periwinkle. Its shell is sometimes yellowish with bands of brown, sometimes white with bands

dinally. The largest genus is *Pomatias,* which is limited to the Mediterranean region.

The family Chondropomidae includes terrestrial snails found in the Caribbean area and northern South America.

The Rissoacea. The superfamily Rissoacea includes a large number of small snails. Some are so tiny that they can hardly be seen without a magnifying glass. *Putilla micrometica,* for example, barely exceeds $\frac{1}{25}$ inch in length. These are cosmopolitan gastropods, common in shallow seas. They consist primarily of marine species, but numerous

The shell of the snail Lamellaria perspicua *(below left) is completely covered by the animal's expanded mantle. Snails of the genus* Lamellaria *are usually larger than their shells.*

A closeup, head-on photo of the snail Cymathium parthenopeum *(below right) shows the bright color and unusual spotty pattern that covers the animal's entire body.*

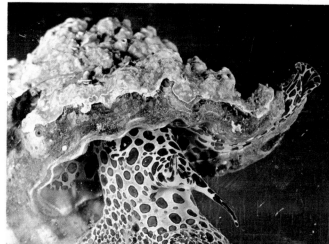

of purple, sometimes purple with bands of brown. This tiny shell, about $\frac{1}{3}$ inch long, is often found entangled in kelp and algae along the continental shelf from Labrador to Long Island Sound. It is also found along the coasts of northern Europe.

L. unifasciata is found along the southern Pacific coast of North America. It is reddish or yellow-brown in color with a brown band around the edge of the shell.

The family Pomatiasidae includes terrestrial snails found in warmer areas. They have no gills, and their foot is split longitu-

specimens live in rivers or brackish water, some in fresh water, and some on land. All are vegetarians. There are more than a dozen families in this group.

The shells of some rissoaceans are shaped like tiny tops, which gives them their common name of spire shells. Others have rather low shells. The outer whorls may be smooth or ornamented with small axial ribs. The color is generally white or yellowish

One of the principal families is the Hydrobiidae, consisting mainly of freshwater species, with some found in brackish water.

Periwinkles (right) are a common sight on rocks along the seacoast. These animals prefer to live out of water; they often congregate in areas reached only by the highest water levels. Periwinkles eat algae, which they scrape from rocks with their radula.

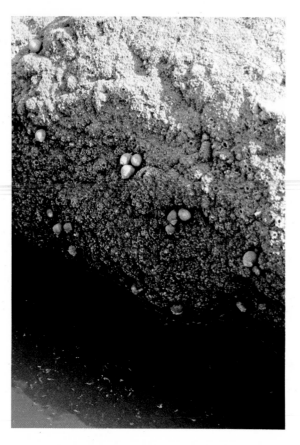

Scattered groups of periwinkles are seen here on a barnacle-covered boulder. Typical of animals that are periodically exposed to the air as the tide ebbs, the periwinkle can shut its shell tightly, thus preventing the loss of body water by evaporation.

In these snails the shell is usually smooth or slightly ornamented. Members of the species *Peringia ulvae* are so abundant in estuaries, brackish ponds, and harbors that they sometimes form strands, or windrows of shells along the beach.

Members of the genus *Hydrobia* are also widely distributed in brackish water. One of the more common spire shells in the United States is *Hydrobia minuta*, a tiny, smooth snail with a surface of shining yellow, found in salt-marsh ponds in the northeast.

Among the interesting members of other families are species of the genus *Pomatiopsis*, which are amphibious in their habits. *P. lapidaria* is found along river banks and under stones in the region east of the Mississippi. It is notable for its ability to crawl on the surface of the water with its shell hanging downward. On land it moves by fastening the tip of its snout to the ground and then drawing the body up to it. Most snails of this genus have gills, but they

If we look at the under-side of the common peri-winkle, Littorina littorea (left), we see its hatchet-shaped foot. Protruding from the upper edge of the foot are two tentacles.

The common periwinkle, Littorina littorea (left), lives in intertidal zones. The thick, squat shell with its sharp peak is easy to recognize. The color may vary from the gray seen here to yellow-brown, olive, or black.

breathe air rather than dissolved oxygen from the water.

Members of the genus *Oncomelania*, found in the Far East, are hosts, or carriers, of the human oriental blood fluke, *Schistosoma japonicum*.

The best known of the land species is *Acme lineata*. It has a small shell a little more than 1/10 inch in length and ornamented by axial lines. It is frequently found under damp stones and in the soil. These are European snails that have lost their gills.

Among the other families the Bulmidae, including the common genus *Bulimus*, are widely distributed in fresh water. They have conical or rounded shells and a calcified operculum. The Rissoidae are small marine snails with conical shells. They are commonly found among clumps of seaweed.

The families Tornidae and Omalogyridae include species that are so small they have been mistaken for Foraminifera.

The Cerithiacea. The superfamily Cerithiacea includes numerous marine and freshwater snails. Their shells are generally high and elongated with many whorls. The opening is sometimes set at an oblique angle, and in some families is slightly flared or may even form a shallow siphonal canal.

Snails of the family Turritellidae are commonly known as the turret shells. Their narrow high shells are pointed at the top. The principal genus of this family is *Turritella*. Its many species are commonly found in temperate and warm seas.

Turritella terebra, the great screw shell, can be 5 inches long and an inch across the base. Its shell is tapered, and each whorl has six raised cords. It is dark brown, brownish-orange, or purplish-brown. Like others of its type, this shell is empty at the top and is divided by a wall at each half-turn. The idea of the helical screw is said to have occurred to the Greek philosopher Archimedes

The spectacular form of this shell makes it a favorite of shell collectors. The shell belongs to the sea snail Murex palmarosae, *found in Ceylon and the Philippines. It reaches a length of about 5 inches.*

after he had studied the shell of the Mediterranean species *T. communis.*

Unlike other families of this group, the sundial shells of the family Architectonicidae have a shell that is flattened—almost disc-shaped. There are about 40 species in this group, which are found primarily in tropical seas. An outstanding beauty is *Architectonica perspectiva* from the Indian and Pacific Oceans. Its shell, in addition to its highly decorative coloration, has a number of whorls that are greatly flattened. The base is completely flat, and an enormous umbilicus allows the inner part of the successive turns to be seen.

Architectonica nobilis occurs in the southern part of the United States from North Carolina down into the Gulf of Mexico; it is also found in the West Indies. Worm shells of the family Vermitidae have tubular shells resembling the tubes of certain polychaete worms. Young snails of this group have a spiral shell, which they firmly attach to a solid substratum. The shell grows, but not in the form of a spiral. Instead, it forms calcareous tubes; only the first few tubes are

The snail Latiaxis pilsbryi *(above), like other members of its genus, has a complex shell form. This species is found off the coast of Japan.*

The snail Murex trunculus *(below), found in the Mediterranean, belongs to the family Muricidae. In ancient days it was collected as a source of murexide. This substance was extracted, oxidized, and transformed into the crimson dye known as Tyrian purple.*

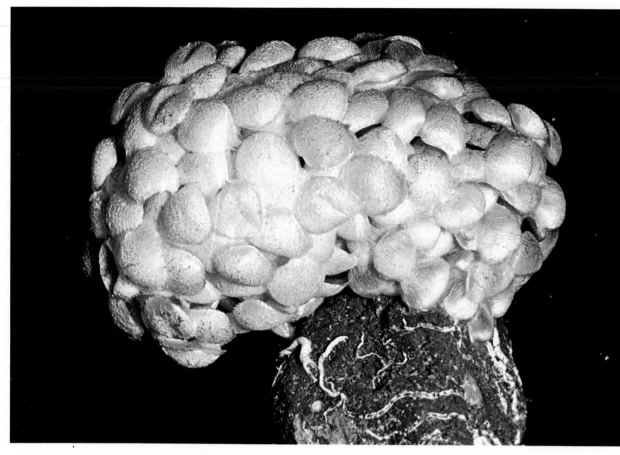

regular, while the rest become contorted and knotted, following an irregular, wormlike course. They are often found in tangled masses, sometimes attached to the shells of other mollusks; in tropical regions they are frequently embedded in coral, rock, and sponges. The shells are sometimes 6 inches long, and the body lengthens to match its shell.

The eyes are located on short tentacles. The foot is small, but the radula is well developed and has a large, trapezoidal tooth at the center and several pairs of lateral teeth.

These animals have separate sexes, and are oviparous or viviparous. However, they do not have copulating organs. The eggs often become attached to the shell of the parent, which explains the chaotic growth of the colony. These warm-sea animals often become so entangled with each other that they form reeflike masses by themselves.

In the family Caecidae, in the course of development, the snails lose an early spiral shell, which is replaced with a tubular one. One member of this family, *Caecum trachea,* is very common. But it is only found by carefully searching the algae in the intertidal zone.

The family Cerithiidae are marine snails found mainly in warm seas. Some are small while others are quite large. The spiraled shell is elongated and has many whorls. It is often decorated with nodules.

In contrast, the members of the related family Cerithiopsidae do not exceed ⅕ inch. They have elongated conical shells and are widely distributed in all seas.

In the fresh waters of tropical and equatorial regions, and occasionally in the temperate zones, there are many snails of the family Melaniidae. Some members of this group bear live young. The genera *Goniobasis* and *Pleurocera* include common freshwater North American species.

Members of the family Planaxidae live only in tropical seas on rocks near the water line. The shell is almost always characterized by a deep inset in the top of the opening. This family contains the single genus *Planaxis*. Females of this group brood their young in an internal pouch.

The family Modulidae includes a few species found in warm seas; a clearly visible tooth on the inner lip helps in recognition.

The family Potamididae consists predominantly of snails that live in rivers and brackish waters. The many species are almost all elongate, with an oval opening and an oblique siphonal canal. *Telescopium telescopium,* common in the Indo-Pacific region, is a large snail. *Cerithidea californica* is found in southern California. *Batillaria minima* is found in Florida and the West Indies.

The Epitoniacea. The superfamily Epitoniacea includes two families—Epitoniidae and Janthinidae. These snails differ greatly in the morphology of their shells, but are very similar in their predatory habits, as shown by their unusual radulas. In these animals the radula has no central tooth. There are a number of teeth, all of the same shape, which become larger towards the edges.

The members of the family Epitoniidae are marine mollusks with extraordinarily graceful shells. They average about an inch in length, although some species are considerably larger; some are minute and live in the depths of the ocean. They are popularly known as wentletraps or staircase shells. Wentletrap is a Dutch word meaning "spiral staircase," and the name is appropriate for these animals with shells that ascend in a winding spire of steplike ribs.

Wentletraps have a shell that is usually white in color. The head has a retractile proboscis, close-set tentacles with eyes at their bases, toothed or spiny jaws, and an elaborate radula. The sexes are distinct. Like the Janthinidae, they are carnivorous and can discharge a purple inklike fluid when disturbed. They are creeping rather than floating animals, however.

The Janthinidae, or violet snails, are remarkable for their ability to float on the surface of the open sea, their natural habitat. The shell of this interesting snail is spherical and extremely delicate, but not light enough for the animal to float without assistance. So it builds a raft by secreting from its foot a mucous band filled with air bub-

The common northern whelk, Buccinum undatum *(above), common along the Atlantic coasts of northern Europe and North America, is a predator of oysters. The shell pattern of rounded ridges crossed by raised lines creates a wavelike effect.*

bles. Its egg capsules are attached to the underside of this raft.

By means of a mechanism not yet understood, this creature can apparently expel the air and sink to the bottom to escape danger, such as a heavy sea, and then return to the surface when the water has become calm. Nevertheless, violent storms sometimes throw thousands of these mollusks onto beaches, painting the sand violet as the shells break, releasing the purple pigment that gives the snails their name.

Violet snails have no eyes. They feed through a prehensile snout that captures polyps and other pelagic creatures. In many areas small jellyfish swarm on the surface of the water in such numbers that the snail only has to reach out with its snout to find a victim. It tears its prey to shreds with a large radula—even though it is a small, blind creature only 1½ inches in diameter, it tackles 5-inch jellyfish with impunity.

The chief enemies of these snails are sea birds who skim the surface, searching for food. However, the protective coloring of the violet-colored shell renders the animal and its little raft almost invisible in the water.

The Eulimacea.

The superfamily Eulimacea contains a large number of small snails, all of them marine species with polished white shells that taper into a slender spire. In some species, the foot secretes a mucus filament that helps the animal to float.

Many species of this group are parasites. They can be found from the Arctic to the tropics, some attached to the shells of bivalves, some to the opercula of other snails, many to the bodies of starfish, sea urchins, and sea cucumbers. One species, fixed on the outside of a sea cucumber, has no foot to move with, but is equipped with a proboscis three times as long as its body, which it uses to tap the skin of its host.

The family Stiliferidae is composed exclusively of species that are parasites of sea cucumbers and other echinoderms. It includes species with flattened or rounded shells as well as some with the more typical elongate shell.

Snails of the family Eulinidae, also parasitic, have small, graceful shells, elongated and pointed, with a clean and shiny surface.

Members of the family Acldidae live at great depths. Their shells are fragile, sometimes almost transparent. *Aclis minima*, which is only about $\frac{1}{50}$ inch in diameter, is probably the smallest species.

The Hipponicacea.

The superfamily Hipponicacea consists of small marine snails. They are divided into two families. The Fossaridae are represented by such spiraled shells as *Fossarus ambiguus*; *F. elegans* and *F. anamola* are species found in the United States. Members of the family Hipponicidae have a cuplike shell that is slightly conical and reinforced internally by a calcareous plate. Members of the species *Hipponix*, which have a cap-shaped shell, attach themselves to a hard substrate when young.

The Calyptraeacea.

Members of the superfamily Calyptraeacea are protandric hermaphrodites—first they function as males; after a transitional period they begin to function as females, and they remain females for the rest of their lives.

The family Trichotropidae, commonly called hairy-keeled snails, are thin, long, and shaped like tops. Their nickname describes the furry skin that covers the surface of the shell. They live in cold seas.

Members of the families Capulidae and Calyptraeidae are limpetlike mollusks that live a sedentary life cemented to stones or shells. The few representatives of the Capulidae have shells that look like conical caps with the peak pulled down to the side. The Hungarian cap, *Capulus hungaricus*, is an example. This mollusk clings to rocks and shells with its sucker foot. It sometimes lives on, but does not injure, such creatures as sea cucumbers. It feeds on minute animal organisms and seaweeds, and reaches a length of between 1 and 2 inches.

Members of the family Calyptraeidae are found in warmer seas. Most have low, conical shells. However, the arched slipper shell, *Crepidula fornicata*, is boat shaped, with a flat head, and an inner cavity partially closed by a horizontal plate. This limy plate, taking up about half the concave interior, looks so much like the quarterdeck of an old sailing vessel that the shell is sometimes called just that—quarterdeck shell—by oystermen who scatter them over the seabed as a "clutch" or "stool" on which to plant seed oysters.

In recent years this snail has spread from the Atlantic coast of North America to the North Sea, and has flourished so profusely there that it has become a nuisance in oyster and mussel banks.

The Strombacea. Members of the superfamily Strombacea are snails of a generous size. They also are creatures of considerable interest, for in addition to an attractive ap-

The whelk Buccinulum corneum *clings to the wall of an aquarium with its large yellow foot. This species is usually found in the Mediterranean. Most members of its family, the Buccinidae, prefer cooler water and are found in northern seas.*

pearance they also exhibit strange behavioral characteristics.

One of the most unusual families is the Xenophoridae, inhabitants of warm and tropical waters. These unique gastropods, whose name means "carrier of strangers," bristle with pebbles, pieces of broken shells, and even whole clam valves, which they cement to their own shells. This ornamentation is not arranged by chance but follows a definite pattern, perhaps serving as camouflage. Apparently there is even an element of choice in the style of decoration. Fossil Xenophoridae have shells lined in precise decorative order resembling coin-shaped Foraminifera. Among living species, some adorn themselves only with rock fragments, while others use only shells.

The family Aporrhaidae is mainly extinct. However, there are a few living species found in the Atlantic and the Mediterranean. These snails are characterized by their expanded outer lip, which sends out a series of toe-like projections. The combination looks like a pelican's webbed foot, and pelican's-foot is what they are often called. Not in Scotland, though. There, at least in days past, the Aporrhaidae went by the ungracious name "blobber-lipt whilk."

Aporrhais pespelecani, common in the Mediterranean, once was eaten only by the poorer classes in Italian coastal towns; today it is considered a delicacy. Pelican's-foot shells and their American relatives, duck's-foot shells (*Aporrhais occidentalis*), have retained the ability to slide in snail fashion across the sea bottom.

The family Strombidae includes the conch shells of the genus *Strombus.* These animals have a most peculiar gait—thrusting the clawlike operculum on the rear of its foot into the sand, the conch literally vaults along, flopping its shell from side to side as it proceeds. A frightened conch can make long leaps and quick turns; if turned on its back, it rights itself by a somersault.

Members of the genus *Strombus* have a sickle-shaped operculum that may be of some use in defense. The queen conch, *Strombus gigas,* is one of the largest mollusks native to the United States. Sometimes it measures a foot in length and weighs 5 pounds. It has a rough exterior, but its flared lip is glossy and rosy pink in color. Semiprecious pink pearls are sometimes found within its mantle folds. When cameos were popular, this shell was a favorite, for under the pink layer is a layer of white.

The many genera in the family Strombidae are all inhabitants of tropical seas; they occur primarily in the Indo-Pacific, with a few species in the West Indies. Some, like the genus *Tibia,* are exquisitely ornamented. *Tibia fusus* from the Philippines and western Pacific, for example, has a long, slender shell with an equally long and even more slender spike projecting from its base. In the rare *Tibia serrata* of the China Sea, the outer lip is profusely decorated with tiny triangular spines. There are other, and more practical, forms of ornamentation, too. In what appears to be a hypothetical case of defensive mimicry, *Strombus mauritianus,* an innocuous species, has a shell closely resembling that of the poisonous *Conus janus,* which lives in the same area.

The shells (right and opposite page, top left) belonged to the sea snail Cancellaria cancellata. *They are called crossbarred shells because they have well-developed vertical crossribs. These snails are vegetarians. They live on sandy bottoms in warm seas.*

Undoubtedly the strangest genus of the family is *Lambis,* composed of about ten species, all from the Indian and Pacific oceans. The lip of this shell, rather than expanding into a wing as in most Strombacea, sends out six, eight, or more long, curved fingers that make the snail look like a great spider or scorpion. From this come the obvious common names, spider shell or scorpion shell. These animals, too, move along the sea bottom by making alternate use of the foot and the operculum. They live along the coast, usually in shallow water.

The Cypraeacea. The superfamily Cypraeacea includes the cowries, which are among the most beautiful shells in the world. These shy, slow-moving mollusks are found in warm seas.

The shell of the money cowrie, *Cypraea moneta,* was once used as money by the natives of the South Seas and tribal chieftains of Africa.

Besides its beauty, the cowrie is remarkable because of the way its shell is formed. When young, the animals have a spiral shell of successive whorls, with a body whorl so wide it almost conceals the spire. A long, thin opening on one side runs nearly the

Snails of the family Olividae, such as Oliva porphyria *(left), have gleaming, naturally polished shells. These snails lay new layers on the outside of the shell rather than on the inside. In addition, they constantly rub the shell with their mantle to keep it free of encrustations.*

entire length of the shell. The outer lip is thin at first, but soon thickens and becomes toothed, with corresponding teeth growing on the inner lip.

The cowrie differs from most other mollusks in the operating procedure of its mantle, which projects in two folds from the opening. The mantle covers the shell, laying down successive layers of enamel on the *outside.* The layers, alternately colored and white, cover more and more of the spire until at last it is completely buried. The shell is then mature, and the mantle puts on a final coat of enamel.

The cowrie's coloration may be monochromatic. Or there may be a pattern of bright spots on the surface, with contrasting bands of colors from the other thin layers shining through. Worth noting, too, is the fact that the coloration of the shell, as striking as it is, cannot compete with the brilliant display of color shown by the cowrie's mantle. The patterns of color vary greatly not only within species but also within individuals. It is little wonder, therefore, that these shells have been sought since antiquity as being among the most admirable jewels offered by nature.

After the shell of the cowrie reaches maturity it stops growing. The animal, however, continues to grow, and this leads to cramped quarters. The cowrie solves the problem in a unique way. The mature shell is quite thick; the animal makes room for itself by secreting an acid that dissolves the inner layers.

Although some taxonomists divide this group into numerous families and genera, others classify all cowries together in the genus *Cypraea.*

Related to the cowry shells, and quite similar to them in many cases, are the shells of the family Ovulidae. The largest living species in this group is *Ovula ovum,* the egg cowry of the Indo-Pacific, which is used as a charm and amulet by many of the Pacific

Islanders. Also placed here are the odd, spindle-shaped shells of the genera *Volva*, *Simnia*, and *Neosimnia*.

Most of these snails live in association with sea whips and sea fans; many of the snails have the same colors as their host. *Cyphoma* of the Atlantic and *Calpurnus* of the Indo-Pacific are genera with shells that are similar to those of the true cowries. The former lives on sea fans, the latter on soft corals.

The family Eratoidae includes snails of the genera *Trivia* and *Erato*. *Trivia* is a large genus; the shells have raised radial ridges. Most species are rather small and are commonly known as coffee-bean shells. The largest species, which occur off South Africa, are just under 1 inch in length. The related genus *Erato* includes smooth-shelled snails.

The Atlantacea. The superfamily Atlantacea includes a number of open-sea mollusks that lead a pelagic life. Because of their floating existence the shell is generally very light and semitransparent; in some the shell is absent altogether. Members of this group have large, well-developed eyes and statocysts.

Members of the family Atlantidae are small and boat-shaped, with very thick shells. On the high seas, extraordinarily large floating shoals of such species as *Atlanta peroni* may be seen. Both the half-inch shells and bodies of these animals are transparent. *Atlanta turriculata*, which has a large head, conspicuous eyes, and a fringed sucker, swims shell downward. As in related species, the foot is dilated into two winglike fins, which are well-adapted for swimming.

The small caplike shell of snails of the family Carinariidae is vitreous, thin, transparent, and very graceful. Active hunters, these snails have a strong fin with a sucker at the end. They are rapid swimmers, darting about and capturing small jellyfish and other sea creatures.

Members of the family Pterotracheidae are the only Mesogastropoda without a shell. Their elongated bodies have a gelatinous appearance. Populating vast areas of warm, tropical seas, their presence contributes to the clouds of plankton on which so many other sea creatures feed.

The Naticacea. Members of the superfamily Naticacea are commonly known as moon shells. These carnivorous snails are widely distributed in all seas.

After choosing a victim, which is usually a bivalve, the predatory snail fastens itself on top of its prey and proceeds to cut a hole through the valve. Its tool is the radula, which it employs in a steady to-and-fro motion, occasionally interrupted by rest periods. Several hours may pass before this task is completed, depending upon the thickness of the shell being drilled. The acid juices emitted by the snail do not, as was once thought, play any part in the boring action; they apparently serve to predigest the soft parts of the prey. Once the circular hole is made in the valve the snail sticks in its long proboscis and sucks out the soft parts.

One of the most remarkable things about this mollusk is the size of its foot—a pad of flesh shaped like an old-fashioned flatiron that may be three times as long as the shell's diameter and half as wide as it is long. People seeing one of these creatures spread out have difficulty believing that the massive foot could ever fit back into what appears to be too-small a shell. Amazingly, though, most species can retract the foot completely into their shells, and can even close the opening perfectly with the horny or calcareous operculum.

There is only one large family of moon shells, the Naticidae. It is divided into numerous subfamilies and genera. The shells, ranging from ¼ to 5 inches, are either spherical or pear-shaped. Colored markings on shells found today often match those on fossil forms, which is unusual. Common genera are *Polinices*, *Natica*, and *Lunatia*.

The Tonnacea. The superfamily Tonnacea includes the tun shells, helmet shells, and others. They are found mainly in warm seas and range from medium to large in size. The capaciousness of their heavy shells makes them useful as containers, and for many years they have been called wine shells and cask shells.

A deep-sea family, the Oocorythidae, includes a few species that live on the bottom at considerable depths. Their spherical shells are rare and in great demand for collections.

The family Cassidae, the helmet shells, have shells that are heavy and thick, sometimes rounded, and sometimes three-cornered. There are about 60 species; the largest, *Cypraecassis rufa* and *Cassis cornuta* of the Indian and Pacific Oceans, are used for making cameos. *Cassis madagas-*

cariensis, a large shell 10 inches or more in length, ranges as far north as the waters off North Carolina, as does *Phalium granulatum*, the granular helmet shell.

Members of the family Cymatiidae are known as the tritons. These animals are voracious predators. Their shells are generally large, with a well-elevated spire, an obvious siphonal canal, and a toothed outer lip. These animals are marked by varices on the turnings of the shell that show where the lip was in earlier stages. The largest genus is *Cymatium;* several of its species are common in the West Indies, as well as in the Indo-Pacific region.

The family Bursidae, the frog shells, has more than 100 species distributed in all warm seas. These sturdy shells, which are medium to large in size, are conical and ornamented with lip varices and sometimes with spines. A special characteristic is the presence of two canals running opposite each other along the opening. Rare at best in

The body of Haminoea hydatis *is too large for its shell, which is partly internal. This mollusk is a member of the order Cephalaspidea. Animals of this order are generally considered to be transitional between the shell-bearing snails and the naked sea slugs.*

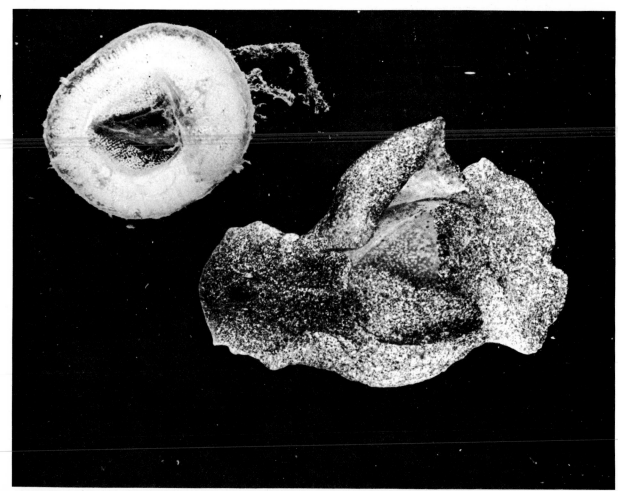

The Neogastropoda

In this third and most highly evolved order of the Prosobranchia, the shell is extended forward in a siphonal canal; in some species the canal is only barely suggested, while in others it is quite pronounced. When present, the operculum is horny. The radula may also be missing; when it is present, it is always narrow and rarely carries more than three teeth. The sexes are separate and a penis is always present in the male. These mollusks, almost exclusively marine, are carnivorous; some contain a poison gland.

northerly waters, *Bursa scrobiculator,* a delicate pink shell that once was common in the Mediterranean, seems in the process of becoming extinct there.

The tun shells of the family Tonnidae are large, but their shells are comparatively thin. The foot can be greatly expanded; there is no operculum. The lip is thick and toothed, as in the genus *Malea,* or simple and sharp, as in *Tonna.* The head of the animal is large, with eyes on the sides of the tentacles. *Tonna galea,* the giant tun shell, is found in shallow waters from North Carolina through the Gulf of Mexico and southward to Brazil. It is also found in the Mediterranean and south to West Africa. Its shell is 6 to 10 inches in height, and much smaller than the animal. The salivary glands of this mollusk contain sulfuric acid, which aids its digestive process. In absolute darkness, it is possible to see a weak luminescence emitted by this snail.

The pear-shaped members of the family Ficidae frequent subtropical seas. *Ficus communis,* common in the Caribbean, is noteworthy for the thinness of its shell, which is almost like parchment. It is one of the common species washed up on the beaches along the Gulf coast of Florida.

The Muricacea. Members of the superfamily Muricacea are commonly called rock shells. They are mostly tropical and subtropical, and can be found from shallow waters to waters some 50 fathoms deep. This superfamily is divided into two families, the Magilidae and the Muricidae.

The gastropods of the small family Magilidae are distinguished by the absence of a radula. Their shells are similar to the spiny shells of the Muricidae, but are generally covered with overlapping calcareous scales. Some species are marvelously formed, especially those of the genus *Latiaxis.* These rare shells from the deep waters off Japan are in great demand by collectors. Their curved spines point upward and their whorls are clearly well-defined. In *L. mawae* the whorls are separated. Some magilids live as parasites on coral.

The Muricidae are carnivorous snails with a long, slim radula. This family contains a far greater number of species than the Magilidae. Pronounced ornamentation of the shell is a characteristic common to all its genera: lip varices, ribs, nodules, spines, ridges, and tubular expansions are all sculptural forms found on many Muricidae. This great variety of decoration, rather than vivid coloring, has made the family a favorite with collectors.

Among the many species are the extremely delicate *Murex tenuispina* of the Indian and Pacific Oceans, ornamented by long, curved spines; the squat, solid shell of *Drupa ricinus* of the Red Sea; the bizarre structures of *Pterynotus pinnatus;* and *Pterynotus elongatus* of the Philippines, *Homalocantha scorpio* of the southern Pacific, *Chicoreus cornuceru* of Australia, *Murex gnatomicus* of Japan, and *Concholepas concholepas* from the west coast of South America. The opening in this last shell is so large that it has sometimes been mistaken for one valve of a strange bivalve.

Although showy coloration is not a strong point of the Muricidae, two species found on the western coast of Panama, *Murex regius* and *Murex radix*, attract attention by their contrasting shades. For combined beauty of color and form, *Murex palmarosae* of Ceylon is among the most splendid.

In the Mediterranean there are species of the genera *Murex* and *Hexaplex* that were prized in antiquity for providing, along with members of the Thaisinae, the famed Tyrian purple dye with which Phoenicians dyed the robes and togas of kings and emperors.

Among oystermen and oysters, several of the rock shells are ranked second only to starfish as enemies. *Hexaplex trunculus,* for example, sometimes called the banded dye murex, seizes the oyster near the hinge, sets its radula on the valve, and rocks back and forth until a tiny hole is drilled through the valve. Then the snail inserts its proboscis and sucks out the liquids. The dead oyster's bivalves open and other scavengers arrive to pick the shell clean. Young snails seem to attack young bivalves, while mature snails choose older victims.

The Buccinacea. The large superfamily Buccinacea is represented in all seas but its members are most common in temperate and colder waters. The Buccinacea of the northern seas show no great variety in form or color. This sometimes constitutes a problem in trying to determine the exact species, particularly in the case of the tinier shells.

The shells of these animals are conical and may be of moderate or great height. There is often spiral sculpturing, and sometimes ribs or tubercles. The lateral teeth of the radula

Among sea slugs of the species Elysia viridis *coloration can vary widely from one individual to another. The most frequent combination, however, is dark green, with spots and stripes of a lighter color. This mollusk of the order Sacoglossa is usually about ¾ of an inch long.*

are generally supplemented by accessory teeth.

The family Pyrenidae, also called Columbellidae, contains the dove shells. They are species with small conical shells; the opening is long and narrow, the toothed outer lip is wrinkled, and the siphonal canal is very short. They are strikingly colored, have a highly polished surface, and are primarily common in warm and temperate seas.

These little animals are usually less than an inch long. In the coastal areas of North America, ranging from Prince Edward Island to the Gulf of Mexico, we find such

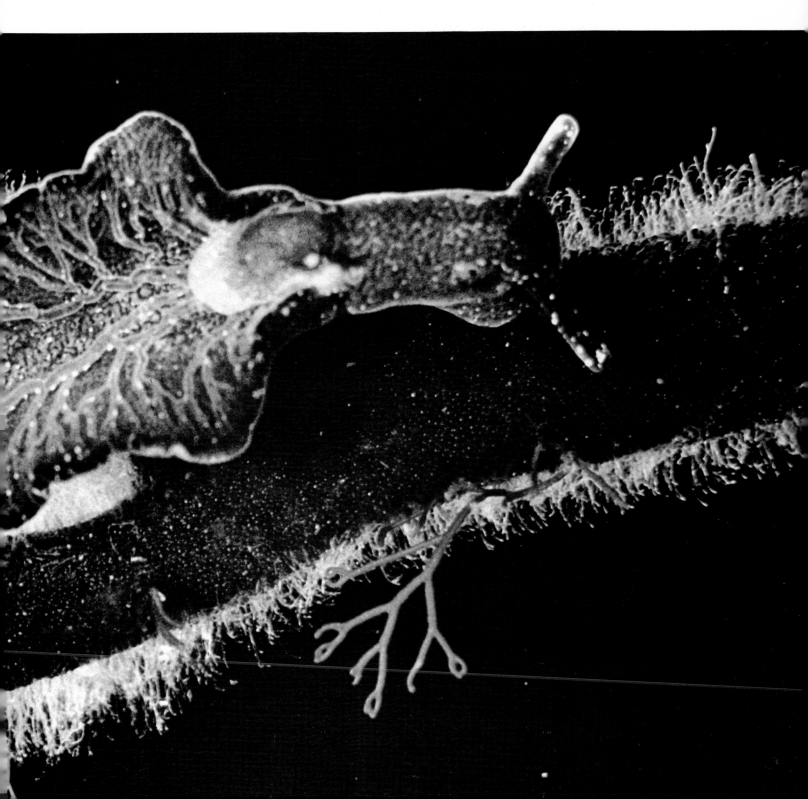

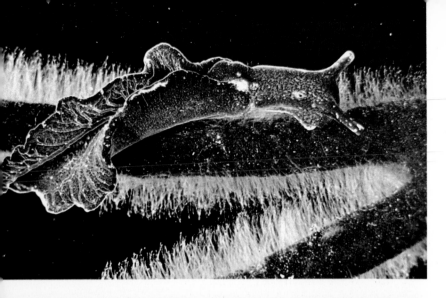

species as *Mitrella lunata*, distinguished by crescent-shaped brown markings on a white ground. The greedy dove shell, *Anarchis avara*, is similar, with a tapering shell that is brown with white dots. It ranges from New Jersey to Florida.

The large family Buccinidae includes the whelks. They have large, thick-walled shells with only a few whorls, which may be smooth or sculptured. It is not unusual to find shells with left-turning spirals in this group. The opening is large, and the siphonal canal may be short or moderately long. Whelks are aggressive, carnivorous animals. They are found as far north as the arctic seas.

Buccinum undatum, frequent in northern seas, owns the dubious honor of rivaling the rock shell *Ocenebra erinacea* as one of the most ferocious enemy of oyster breeders. This voracious predator has a white body streaked and blotched with black. Below a prominent spire there are usually six whorls, gray in color, and twelve rounded ridges crossed by raised lines. The combination creates a wavy effect, which accounts for the common name of the animal, the waved whelk. Its shell is usually 3 inches in height, although larger specimens have been found. This whelk lays eggs in yellowish capsules about the size of a split pea. A mass of egg capsules, picked up on the beach, looks like a coarse sponge; at sea, sailors are reputed to scoop them up for use in place of soap to wash their hands, referring to them as "sea-wash balls."

This whelk has been a staple food item for centuries in northern Europe, but has little market value in North America. A nuisance to fishermen because of its practice of stealing bait from lobster pots and cod lines, it is used as bait for codfish.

Other common genera in this family are *Volutopsius* and *Neptunea*, which are found in colder waters; and *Cantharus*, *Engina*, and *Macron*, which inhabit warm waters.

The family Melongenidae, related to the whelks, is represented only in warm seas. The members include the largest living gastropod, *Syrinx aruanus* of Australia, an animal that exceeds 24 inches in length.

The family Nassaridae includes gastropods popularly known as dog whelks, basket shells, or mud snails. Common throughout the world, they are scavengers in shallow coastal areas, feeding not only on living prey but also on all kinds of dead and decaying animal matter. Thus, they help keep the waters clean.

The shells of these snails is conical with spiral sculpturing. There is a short siphonal canal and a relatively small opening. These snails may be captured in large numbers clinging to fishermen's baskets, for the odor of the bait inside is picked up quickly by their remarkably keen sense of smell. Like most scavengers, these hungry animals usually show up when food is available, crawling over each other in their eagerness to get at the prey.

The most important genus of the family is *Nassarius*. It includes many species found in all seas. Snails of this genus are characterized by the presence of a long proboscis, a very small operculum, and a foot that can be expanded; they also have two horns at the anterior end and two cirri at the posterior end.

The largest species in the family is the channeled basket shell, *Nassarius fossatus*, from California, which is usually 1 to 2 inches long. East coast representatives include the wornout basket shell, *Ilynassa obsoleta*, whose shell is eroded at the apex like a basket with a damaged bottom. This is the common mud snail found along the Atlantic seaboard. The habitat of the dog whelk, or common nassa, *Nassarius vibex*, is the same as that of *I. obsoleta*, but this animal prefers sandy bottoms to mud flats.

Snails of the family Fasciolariidae are large creatures with thick-walled, spindle-shaped shells and a sharp spire. There is a moderate-length or long siphonal canal and a very long proboscis. The whorls of the shell are marked by wide spiral bands, and the members of this family are therefore called band shells. There are two subfamilies: the Fusinae, with a long canal and a smooth inner lip; and the Fasciolarinae, with a shorter canal and the suggestion of spiral folds on the inner lip.

These snails are widespread throughout the waters of warm seas. Slow moving, they crawl about on mud flats or bury all but the tip of their spire in the sand. They boast conspicuously handsome shells, and some are among the largest of all the gastropods.

Pleuroploca gigantea, for example, called the giant band shell or the horse conch, is the second largest gastropod. This magnificent shell, which grows to 2 feet in length, is the largest snail known in North American waters, where it ranges along the coast from North Carolina to Mexico. Its whorls, usually ten in number, taper to form an elongated spire. It is yellowish in color under a horny brown epidermis, and the aperture is lined with bright orange-red. The animal it-

The mollusks on the facing page belong to the order Sacoglossa. There is a major difference between the two species. Elysia viridis (top) has no dorsal papillae. These organs, which look like bunches of short tentacles, appear on Placida dendritica (bottom). The papillae function as a respiratory device.

The unusual snail Aplysia rosea *(left) has a small, translucent shell that is completely hidden in the animal's long, meaty body. Commonly known as a sea hare, it belongs to the order Aplysiacea. In the spring many sea hares can be found along the Mediterranean coast.*

self is a brilliant red and a "fighter" because of its size and weight.

The tulip shell, *Fasciolaria tulipa,* is a smaller but extremely handsome shell, similar to a tulip in form if not always in color. From a swollen center, graceful whorls taper to a sharp spire and a straight canal. The thin lip is finely scalloped; the inner lip has three folds. Coloration and design vary greatly, but spirals and blotches of light colors over warm grays and uniform browns are common. This species, from 4 to 8 inches in length, ranges from the Carolinas and the Gulf of Mexico to the West Indies.

The Fusininae are particularly attractive because of their graceful, cigar-shaped shells. The needle fusus, *Dolicholatirus acus,* of the China Sea, is the slimmest and most graceful member of this group.

The giant of the family Fasciolariidae, *Syrinx aruanus,* is from Australia. Specimens as long as 2 feet can be found.

The Volutacea. The superfamily Volutacea includes five families that contain some of the most beautiful shells imaginable. There are thousands of marine species in the group, denizens of the warm seas. The inner lip is frequently ornamented by spiral folds. In some species there is a thin, small operculum.

Members of the family Olividae are commonly known as olive shells. These polished shells have a low spire. The body whorl is long; the opening is narrow. There are great color variations even among members of the same species. This group inhabits warmer waters and is common in the Indo-Pacific. As in the Cypraeidae, the Olividae wrap the mantle around the shell to deposit new layers, giving the outside of the shell a splendid shiny smoothness. Striking patterns of color often decorate this gleaming surface.

Oliva sayana, the lettered olive shell, is generally a bluish-gray covered with fine markings in brown and pink.

Perched atop a voluminous body, the disklike shell of the Umbraculum mediterraneum *is hardly useful as a protective device. The animal finds food peaceably, by grazing on sponges or deposits. Its broad radula bears a record number of teeth—150,000.*

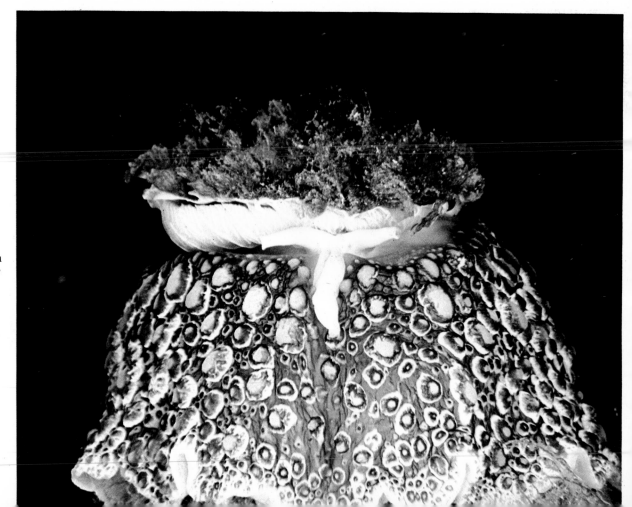

The smallest animals in this family, the genus *Olivella,* are called rice shells. Unlike *Oliva,* they have an operculum. *Olivella mutica,* the little olive, is the most common. Only ½ inch long, it is colorful and has been used to make necklaces.

Olivella biplicata, the two-plated olive shell of the West Coast, is sometimes blue, sometimes white, sometimes dark brown or olive green. Strung together in long strands, they were once used as shell money by the Indians; later, Victorian decorators used them for bead curtains.

Members of the family Mitridae are known as miter shells. They have elegant turreted shells with a pointed spire and pronounced characteristic folds on the inner lip. A few species range as far north as the Mediterranean and the southern shores of the United States, but this family occurs primarily in the Pacific and Indian Oceans.

The episcopal miter, *Mitra mitra,* is creamy white overlaid with orange spots in regular rows. The papal miter, *Mitra papalis,* is thick, stout, and covered with crimson spots on white. The pontifical miter, *Mitra stictica,* is white with orange spots; its whorls are crowned with a spiral row of erect, triangular cusps.

Members of the family Vasidae are widely distributed in tropical seas. Their heavy conical shells are low or moderately high with protuberances on the whorls. The most important genera are *Vasum* and *Turbinella.* Snails of the genus *Vasum,* such as *V. rhinoceros* of East Africa, are squat and robust and have a moderately long siphonal canal. Members of the genus *Turbinella* have a longer siphonal canal.

Few shells are as gaudy as those of the family Harpidae, which includes about ten tropical species. Numerous axial ribs stretch from spire to base like the strings of a harp, and the spaces between are often adorned with geometric patterns of rare elegance. There is no operculum in the harp shells perhaps for the simple reason that it could never be closed—the shell is so much smaller than the animal that head, tentacles, and the crescent-shaped foot still protrude when the snail is drawn inside as far as it will go. The color scheme of the fleshy parts is as bright as that of the shell.

Members of the family Volutidae have a wide distribution, but there are only a few species on the coasts of North America. Their shells are moderate to large in size, and are shaped like elongated cones. There is a siphonal canal of medium length, a large foot, and a small proboscis. In most species there is no operculum.

The subfamily Volutinae includes the fantastic species *Voluta musica* of the West Indies, whose shell is adorned with sets of lines and dots that look like reproductions from a sheet of music. This West Indian shell is one of the few volute species possessing an operculum. Eggs of the genus *Cymbium* hatch inside the mother's body, and the young grow a thin shell before they leave their maternal shelter. The shells of this subfamily are shorter and wider than those of the other groups.

Members of the subfamily Scaphellinae always have an inner lip with obvious folds. The shell has an elongated, graceful shape. In most other respects, the Scaphellinae are similar to the Volutinae.

The subfamily Haliinae has a single species, *Halia priamus*, from northwest Africa. This interesting animal does not display characteristics paralleling those of the other family members, and systematists debated long before assigning it to the volutes. One unusual fact about it, which has no bearing on its classification, is that its shell exudes

The Glossodoris luteorosea *in this picture looks like an oddly shaped submarine aglow with lighted portholes. A small nudibranch, it measures less than a half-inch in length.*

lives in large colonies at shallow depths on sandy bottoms or under stones.

The most interesting species are found along the coast of West Africa. One of these, *Persicula cingulata,* is very elegantly patterned. Its spire is sunken, and the opening extends to the top of the shell. Other genera include *Marginella,* which has a true spire; *Prunam,* with a very short spire; and *Hyalina,* whose spire is almost nonexistent.

The Conacea. The superfamily Conacea includes the cone shells and others. Their radula is different from that of other groups. They also have a long proboscis. Snails of this group are carnivorous. Most of the Conacea secrete a poisonous saliva that is injected into the prey with a tooth. The toxin of some species is dangerous to man.

The very large family Turridae contains several thousand species, which are widely distributed in warmer waters. The shells are

The sea slug Polycera elegans *(left) is an attractive nudibranch, with an unusual shape and colorful markings. It lives in shallow water along the Atlantic coast.*

The sea slug Okenia quadricornis *(below) is about ½ inch long. It lives along the shores of Great Britain.*

a sweet, pleasant odor that lasts for a considerable period of time.

Snails of the family Cancellariidae, the cross-barred or nutmeg shells, have heavily developed ribs crossing their shells. The shells are conical and quite small. The siphonal canal is short. There is no operculum to close the shell opening. Instead, the foot always has a coating of sand on the bottom, so that when it retreats into the shell, the opening seems to be partly filled with sand —a device apparently designed to make enemies believe the shell is uninhabited.

The shells of the family Marginellidae are small and have a porcelaneous texture, for this animal also polishes the outer surface with its mantle. The spire of these shells is generally low or sunken in. Most species are less than an inch in length, but the bubble margin shell, *Closia bullata,* from South America, grows to more than 3 inches. Found in tropical and subtropical waters, it

conical and moderately high with various types of sculpturing. The length of the siphonal canal varies with the species from short to long. Among the common genera are *Daphnella; Clavus,* which have a tall, longitudinally ribbed shell; *Crassispira,* which have an elongated opening; *Mangelia,* with no operculum; and *Clavatula,* which are heavy, glossy shells from West Africa.

Typically, the exotic species from the Indian and Pacific Oceans are the most elegant. *Tatcheria mirabilis* is a showy species from Japan. Species inhabiting the waters of North America are generally of somber colors, and rarely exceed ¾ inch in length.

The large family Conidae includes almost 700 species, all members of the single genus *Conus*. Most species inhabit tropical waters but a few are found in temperate zones. Mollusks of this group have a characteristic cone-shaped shell with a large, elongated body whorl and a long, narrow opening; there is a relatively low spire. *Conus textile*, the cloth-of-gold cone, has longitudinal zigzag lines of dark brown splashed with yellow; these lines form three bands of color on a white background and are divided into triangular patches by brown lines.

Most cone shells are common within their range. There are, however, about 20 species that are very rare. In fact, the most famous shell in the history of conchology is *Conus gloriamaris*, the glory of the sea. Although discovered over 150 years ago, only about 250 perfect specimens have been collected. Although it is not particularly beautiful it is very valuable because it is so rare.

The most sharply pointed mollusk shells belong to the members of the family Terebridae, the auger shells. The spire is long, slender, and coiled, with a sharp apex and many whorls. The surface of the shell may be smooth or sculptured with low ribbing. More than 200 species are distributed in all the warm seas, but they are especially common in the Indo-Pacific area. These animals generally live in shallow coastal waters. Although they have a poison gland they are not very aggressive. A few members of the family are found in North American waters, but they are small and dull-colored compared with their large, highly colored relatives to the south, which are usually polished and mottled or banded with shades of brown on a pale background.

The spotted auger shell, *Terebra maculata*, is a good representative of the tropical types. Heavy and solid, with many closely wound flat whorls, it forms a 6-inch needle cone of elegance and mathematical exactness. Appearing on a ground color of creamy white are two bands of colored spots, the upper one chestnut, the lower, purple or slate gray-blue, separated by a line of dark brown or black. In the past Polynesians ate the flesh of this graceful snail and fashioned the shells into chisels to carve their canoes.

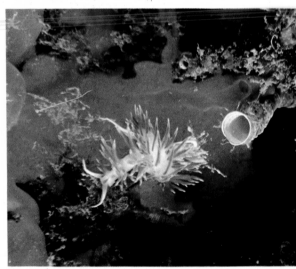

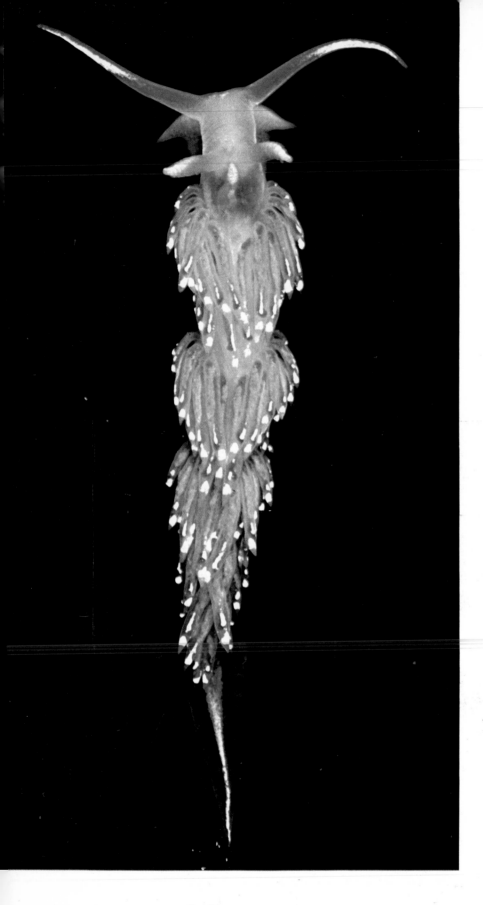

The Cephalaspidea

Cephalaspidea is the largest order in the subclass Opisthobranchia. It contains the shell-bearing sea slugs. In this order the dorsal surface of the head of the mollusk has an expanded thickening called the *cephalic shield*. This shield may have formed as the result of the welding together of the tentacles. There is a flat-soled foot used for creeping. The foot has large, almost winglike lateral extensions called *parapodia*, which can be used in swimming.

In most cases, but not all, the shell is large enough to house the animal. The Cephalaspidea are the only opisthobranchs with a spiral, conical, external shell. However, even in this order there is a tendency for the shell to be reduced and the body to be enclosed in the body whorl. In such cases the shell is egglike. The right gill, contained within the mantle cavity, functions for respiration.

The family Acteonidae is a link between this order and the Prosobranchia, for its members still have some of the anatomical characteristics of the latter. They retain a spiral shell that covers the body and into which the animal can withdraw. They have a well-developed spire, a horny operculum, a toothed radula, and a twist in the visceral loop of the nervous system.

Among the most common species of this family is *Acteon tomatilis,* which inhabits shallow European waters. It lives burrowed in the sand just below the surface, and uses its cephalic shield for digging.

The family Ringiculidae was extensively represented throughout the Tertiary period; only a few living species are known. In this family there are small teeth on the inner lip of the shell. When these animals are burrowed in the mud they use part of their wide cephalic shield to form a respiratory siphon, which extends up to the surface. The family contains the single genus *Ringicula.*

Members of the family Scaphandridae are known as canoe shells. They have external shells that are reduced to an oval with a sunken spire—the animal can only partially withdraw into it. *Scaphander lignarius,* a burrower in muddy bottoms, partially wraps its ample soft parts around its thin, ochre-colored shell.

In the family Philinidae, the calcareous shell is completely covered by the mantle. The shell is very thin, made up mostly of the last turn. Compared to the total size of the creature, the shell has an enormous opening. Apparently this shell, which sometimes is entirely absent, is in the last stages of reduction.

During the day members of the genus *Philine* stay burrowed in the sand. At night they come almost to the surface and move along covered by a thin layer of sand and mucus. *Philine sinuata* is a tiny, sluglike animal, about $\frac{1}{12}$ inch long, with a rudimentary concealed shell that is practically transparent. This mollusk is blind and burrows in mud and slime to find even tinier creatures, which it swallows whole.

Members of the family Bullidae are commonly known as bubble shells. The ample, oval shell has a sunken spire. The body is large and fleshy and can be withdrawn into the shell. The mantle has flaps that are used for swimming. The diet consists primarily of small bivalves and snails.

The cloudy bubble shell, *Bulla gouldiana* has the appearance and fragility of a bird's egg. Its habitat is southern California. The largest bubble shell, *Bulla ampulla* from the Pacific, is the size of a hen's egg.

Species of the family Hydatinidae have shells similar to those of the Bullidae, but they are thinner and are often covered by a marvelously colored skin.

The sea slug Facelina coronata *(opposite page) is common in the cooler waters of the Atlantic, off the coast of Great Britain. These animals can attain a length of an inch or more.*

Although they look almost identical, these sea slugs belong to two different species. Coryphella verrucosa *(far left) is an Atlantic species slightly more than an inch long.* Coryphella lineata *(near left) is a Mediterranean species slightly less than an inch long.*

The Sacoglossa

The order Sacoglossa includes some species that have a shell, some in which there is no shell, and a unique family of gastropods whose members are bivalves—that is, they have two shells.

In 1959, two Japanese biologists, S. Kawaguti and K. Baba, discovered an extraordinary creature. Formed like a slug, it had a head, tentacles, and a radula. But around its body was a bivalve shell equipped with an adductor muscle. The two scientists named the strange animal *Tamanovalva limax*; later, the name was changed to *Berthelinia limax*. In 1875 another malacologist, Crosse, had collected some empty valves of this animal and quite logically at-tributed them to a new genus of bivalves, which he named *Berthelinia*. Taxonomists today place these unusual gastropods in the family Juliidae.

The other members of this order are generally divided into two groups. The first group consists of gastropods that have a shell. This shell, however, is too small to contain the animal. These animals have parapodia on the foot, but they lack external respiratory projections called cerata. The most common genera of this group are *Oxynoe* and *Lobiger*.

The second group consists of gastropods that have no shell. However, many of them do have cerata. Among the most common genera are *Elysia, Caliphylla, Limapontia, Stiliger*, and *Alderia*.

The land snail Helicigona zonata *is active at night. This photo was taken just after sunset as the snail was beginning to search for a meal of fungi and other plant matter.*

The Anaspidea

The order Anaspidea includes mollusks that are popularly known as sea hares. This group of relatively large gastropods contains the superfamily Aplysiacea, which is divided into two families—Aplysiidae, which includes most sea hares, and Akeridae, with only one genus.

These snails swim about among the seaweed using their broad side flaps as fins. A siphonal fold in the mantle brings water to the gill, which is under the small shell. Glands under the skin of the mantle contain a foul-smelling liquid—a black or purple ink—which the animal spurts into the water to hide its movements when danger approaches.

Sea hares inhabit several depths during their life-span. They move into deep water while they are growing, returning to the shallow water where they were born at maturity. Swimming about among the seaweeds and anemones on which they feed, they take on protective coloring. At breeding time they flock together in large colonies, and lay their eggs among the seaweeds in gelatinous, threadlike cases.

Sea hares of the family Aplysiidae are commonly found in tropical and subtropical waters. They are characterized by the presence of a reduced shell that is in the form of a flat plate. The lobes of the mantle almost completely cover this plate. The head end has a pair of regular tentacles and a pair of specialized rolled or rabbit-ear tentacles called *rhinophores;* there is also a pair of eyes. A neck connects the head to the trunk. These sea hares may be 6 inches or more in length. They have the appearance of a mass of mottled purple or brown jelly.

The family Akeridae includes the single genus *Akera.* These mollusks have a shell but it is not large enough for the animal to withdraw into it. There are large parapodia and a mantle tentacle.

The drawings (above) show the location of the pneumostoma, or respiratory pore, of two land slugs: a member of the family Limacidae (top) and a member of the family Arionidae (bottom).

The land snail Helix lucorum *(top left) looks very much like the popular edible snail* Helix pomatia. *The dark bands on its shell are a distinguishing characteristic.*

The Elysiacea and Polybranchiata. The superfamilies Elysiacea and Polybranchiata are composed of small animals, extremely attractive in color, that are found frequently among algae.

Elysia chlorotica is common along the northeastern coast of the United States. This animal has a clearly defined head, rounded and somewhat bilobed in front. A neck connects it to the body, which has lateral ridges formed into finlike expansions for swimming. Extending forward from the head are two delicate tentacles, with eyes set just behind them. The emerald green body is marked by white spots and a scattering of red dots. It is a little more than 1½ inches in length.

Elysia catula is more sea-green in color, with a shading into brown toward the head. A white streak marks the median line between the tentacles, which are short and blunt. Whitish spots appear behind each tentacle and between the fins, which are used in swimming.

Members of the genus *Caliphylla* have two rows of numerous, flattened cerata on the dorsal surface. In *Limapontia* there are neither parapodia or cerata; these slugs look almost like flatworms. Species of the genus *Alderia,* along with *Limapontia,* are often found in brackish waters.

The Thecosoma and Gymnosoma

These two orders formerly were classified together in the single group Pteropoda. Although they are now divided into two separate orders their members are still referred to as pteropods. They are small, free-swimming animals of the open sea, reaching shore only by accident. The strong winglike parapodia are used in swimming. The pteropods are all hermaphroditic.

These animals live in vast communities in all seas, feeding on microscopic mollusks and crustaceans. The arctic species are the most colorful. They rise to the surface at twilight and swim about, flapping their fins in lively fashion, which accounts for their popular name, sea butterflies.

Members of the order Gymnosoma do not have shells as adults. Also, there is no mantle cavity. The body is divided into a head and a long, broad trunk. The head has two pairs of tentacles, two eyes, a foot, and parapodia. In some families there are specialized devices around the mouth that are used for catching prey.

Species of the family Clionidae lack gills; respiration takes place through the skin or through dorsal cerata. They have a distinct head; ear-shaped tentacles that contain the eyes. Although adults are entirely naked, embryos have shells for a short while.

Clione limacina, about 1½ inches in length, is found in northern waters. It has a transparent body that is colored light blue. Swimming in great schools, these animals sometimes tint the water for miles. They are a prime food of certain whales.

The family Pneumodermatidae is the only one in this order whose members have suckered arms. The family Cliopsidae contains only one genus, *Cliopsis,* which has a reduced anterior region. Genera of the family Notobranchaeidae have short necks. In the Thliptodontidae the head and trunk

regions are of equal length; the parapodia are in the middle of the body. Species of the families Anopsiidae and Laginiopsiidae have no prey-catching devices around the mouth and the radula is also absent.

The Thecosoma have light-colored shells that are nearly or totally transparent. In most the shell is calcareous; in some it is coiled in a spiral. There may also be an operculum. They have no definite head, no eyes, and only one pair of tentacles. The radula contains only three teeth in each row. The Thecosoma are vegetarians. These small creatures represent an important element in the ocean plankton.

The single genus *Spiratella* of the family Spiratellidae has a spiral shell and an operculum. There is no gill. In the Cavolinidae the shells vary considerably in shape. In this group there is a large gill.

In the remaining four families there is a snout, or proboscis, formed by fusion of parts of the foot and parapodia. These families are Peraclididae, Procymbuliidae, Cymbuliidae, and Desmopteridae.

The freshwater snail Planorbis corneus, *of the family Planorbidae, has orange coloring. The delicate shell is marked with fine, close-set narrow lines. Members of this family can be found in many areas where there is stagnant or slow-running water.*

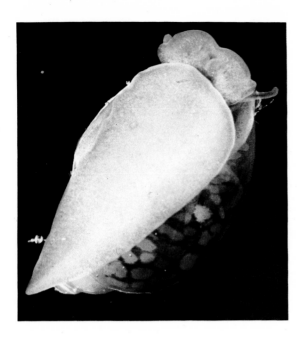

The Notaspidea

Members of the order Notaspidea usually have a shell and a gill but parapodia are absent. This order includes two families.

The Umbraculidae are animals that attain a length of about 8 inches. In the genus *Tylodinella* the animal can withdraw into its shell; in *Tylodina* the caplike shell is too small to enclose the animal. In the best-known species, *Tylodina citrina*, the shell has a characteristic sulfur-yellow color. As in *Tylodina* the small disc-shaped shell of *Umbraculum* cannot cover the animal. Members of this genus have a particularly large, heavy foot covered with tubercles.

In the family Pleurobranchidae the translucent, platelike shell is covered by the mantle. However, in some species there is no shell. These animals are large, with an oval shape. The body is heavy, the head is big, and the foot is highly developed. On the head is a structure known as the *frontal sail. Bouvieria aurantiaca* is a typical, though comparatively rare, coastal species. Representatives have been found measuring up to a foot in length.

The Nudibranchia

Many of the mollusks bear fitting, fanciful, and beautiful names. Few are as inappropriately named as the lovely, graceful Nudibranchia. Their name: naked sea slugs. There is no doubt that they do resemble the slimy land slug in body shape and lack of shell. But here the similarity ends. For the nudibranchs are clothed in striking colors and body decorations that seem to have been created in some marine fairyland.

The members of this order are easily recognized. They have a sluglike shape, there are cerata or other growths on the back that function as respiratory organs, and their coloring is bright. Adults never have a shell; the coiled shell occurring in embryos is discarded soon after birth. They have no mantle cavity or internal gill, but they do possess both jaws and a radula. On the head there are usually two pairs of tentacles. The body, which is externally bilaterally symmetrical, includes the foot, visceral organs, and mantle.

Nudibranchs are marine mollusks that live close to the coast. They are numerous and inhabit all the seas of the world. With some rare exceptions these animals are small, seldom exceeding 2 inches in length. Regardless of size, few animals move through the water more gracefully. Gliding along with an undulating motion, nudibranchs swim among the stems of seaweeds in the shallow waters they inhabit, feeding on algae, sponges, jellyfish, and anemones.

Nudibranchs are hermaphroditic. They lay their eggs in a gelatinous cord, fixing one end of the whitish band to a support and wrapping it around in spiral fashion; in other cases they festoon the branches of seaweeds with the eggs and cord. While laying its eggs, the animal turns in a clockwise spiral movement, thereby forming the eggs into a compact mass. The process of laying eggs lasts for several hours.

A view through an aquarium glass shows the snail Physa acuta. *It is sometimes called the pouch snail or golden pippin. An active species, it glides under the water's surface, drops to the bottom, and climbs back up on threads of mucus.*

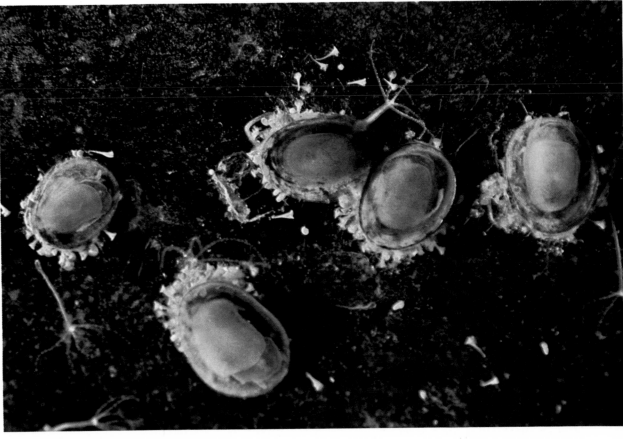

Some species attain sexual maturity in an astonishingly short time. *Aeolis amoena,* for example, is capable of depositing a band of eggs within ten days after it is born. On the other hand, the life span of nudibranchs is generally short. In rare cases the animal may live as long as two years; an average life span for most species, however, is about twelve months.

One remarkable characteristic of these animals is their propensity for autonomy, the voluntary self-amputation of parts of the body to escape danger. When fishes or other predators seize a nudibranch by its showy dorsal appendages, the mollusk immediately detaches this part of its body and hurries on its way.

The coloring of nudibranchs also usually has a defensive purpose. The mantle edge of *Idalina elegans,* for example, is fringed with numerous orange filaments tipped with yellow. This animal generally nests in the body of a tunicate, allowing its filaments to jut out between layers. So closely does it resemble a sea anemone with stinging tentacles extended that few fish will venture near it.

Other nudibranchs have sheaths at the tips of the tubular growths on their back that are lined with special stinging cells. If a fish tries to attack a stinging nudibranch such as *Aeolis,* it is quickly stung. People with salt-water aquariums have noticed that this mollusk is left in peace even when impounded in close quarters with such voracious crustaceans as crabs. One of the more remarkable events in nature is the manner in which *Aeolis* obtains its stingers. When it eats a jellyfish or anemone, it somehow preserves their stinging cells and draws them up into the cells on its back, where they are adapted for the mollusk's own use.

The nudibranchs form a large order, which is divided into 4 suborders, 47 families, and a very large number of genera and species. Only some of the more common groups are discussed below.

Among the family Doridae is the fairly common sea lemon, or warty slug, of the Mediterranean, *Archidoris tuberculata*. This large yellow species resembles a lemon cut in half lengthwise. Its back is warty with limy spicules, gill plumes are arranged in a rosette at the posterior end, and two leaf-like tentacles appear in front. This slowly gliding creature is camouflaged by its resemblance to the crumb-of-bread sponges on which it feeds. Its egg ribbon, which it glues to a rock, is wound into a wonderful rosette form. The young have a nautiloid shell.

Members of the family Platydoridae have a flat shape and a leathery consistency. The mantle is often smooth and much larger than the foot. Most of the species live in tropical waters. *Platydoris argo,* red with its gills alternately white and brown, is well known in the Mediterranean.

In the family Glossodoridae the mantle is smooth and translucent. The radula has teeth with serrated edges. *Glossodoris gracilis* is quite a small species, measuring less than ½ inch, but it is colored gorgeously in blue with yellow edges and a white dorsal line. Less common is the related species *Glossodoris valenciennesi.* Its coloring is similar to that of *G. gracilis* but it may reach a length of 5 inches, which ranks it with the largest of the nudibranchs. Many other species of this genus are common in warmer waters.

The Discodoridae have a vaguely rectangular form and granular mantle; the teeth of the radula are hooklike. The Lamellidoridae also have hooked teeth, and contractile gills around the anus. *Lamellidoris bilamellata,* the largest species of the

family, is so common in the Atlantic that in certain seasons its colonies cover the beaches. These animals are encircled by rounded tubercles and are of a faded olive-green color.

The family Arminidae contains large species, some longer than 4 inches long, that live in the open sea. These animals do not have gills or cerata plumes on their backs but breathe through branchial plates under the mantle. A noteworthy species is *Armina tigrina,* which has a pink background with zebra stripes on the back, foot, and the front of the head.

Tritonia hombergi of the family Tritoniidae is one of the largest of all nudibranchs, attaining a length of as much as 8 inches. It lives along the Atlantic and Mediterranean coasts. It generally is a greenish color marbled with brown. In addition to *Tritonia,*

The large land slug Arion ater *(above) feeds on a tomato. This species, which can reach a length of 6 inches, causes serious damage in gardens and farms. They are common in central Europe and are extending their range.*

another common genus of this family is *Marionia.*

Externally, the family Dendronotidae, the bushy-backed slugs, resemble the Tritoniidae. In both groups the rows of branching, tree-like cerata on their backs make them look like miniature, mobile forests. *Dendronotus arborescens* (or *frondosus*) carries seven pairs of translucent cerata. The blunt head has about six branching appendages extending forward. Its color runs from brown to red to yellowish, mottled with spots of yellow, white, or red.

The family Fimbriidae includes sea slugs in which the anterior end is expanded. *Fimbria fimbria* exceeds 8 inches in length and has a frontal veil almost as wide as the animal is long, which gives it an unmistakable appearance. This animal, white with

There are no appendages except for a pair of rhinophores. The Cutonidae, on the other hand, are small nudibranchs with numerous, spindle-shaped cerata distributed over the back. Common among algae accumulations is *Trinchesia foliata,* a tiny mollusk colored olive-green and striped with yellow.

The most important genus in the Facelinidae, a family of many species, is *Facelina.* These animals have long, thin bodies, long mouth appendages, platelike rhinophores, and two or three rows of cerata along the sides of the body. Identification of the species is based almost entirely on color. A gaudy representative is *Facelina drummondi,* an almost transparent animal whose reddish visceral mass shows through its external surface. Its cerata are dark brown, its head is red, and its tail area is striped with blue.

This land slug of the genus Milax *belongs to the family Limacidae. A plant-eating animal, it can be seen in woods and gardens after rains or at night when dew begins to form.*

black and red spots, swims by contracting its entire body and by beating the ample sheaths in which its olfactory tentacles are enclosed. To capture the crustaceans and fish on which it feeds, it pushes the frontal veil forward and out like a net.

In contrast to this hunter, members of the family Scyllaeidae live on floating algae. These mollusks are characterized by winglike expansions at the sides of the back.

The Phylliroidae are pelagic nudibranchs. Their greatly reduced body folds, without gills, are translucent and laterally flattened.

The appearance of *Caloria maculata* is perhaps even more elegant. Its clear body has two oval spots of brilliant orange in front of the tentacles, red spots of visceral matter evident through its body, circles of white dots at the ends of the cerata filaments, and an overall cast of iridescent blue.

The family Dotonidae consists of small species with only a single series of lobed filaments along the body. The largest genus of this group is *Doto.* In the Flabellinidae, the two pairs of tentacles are unequal in length and the front angles of the foot are prolonged. The beautiful *Flabellina affinis* is colored a delicate violet and its bright-red liver shows through its transparent body. The violet intensifies in the head and the tentacles, where it is dotted with brown.

The family Aeolidiidae includes *Spurilla neapolitana,* which has a light pinkish body brightened by green patterns. *Berghia coerulescens* is yellow with iridescent blue reflections.

Aeolis papillosa, the plumed sea slug, is common on both the European and North American shores of the Atlantic. Its back is covered with cerata, the brightly colored papillae that serve as gills. The cerata tend to part in the middle and fall away to the sides. The body, 4 inches long at maturity, is broad in front and tapers to a point behind. The coloring is usually orange or gray spotted with white, purple, or green. However, this slug also takes on the color of the animals it eats; particles of the prey's body, such as stinging cells, permeate the slug's system and are drawn up into the cerata, changing the color.

The Glaucidae are pelagic nudibranchs that feed on velellas, a type of bluish coelenterate. The filaments on the sides of their bodies open like fans, making it easy for them to float or swim. *Glaucus atlanticus,* the only species in this family, is blue, striated with yellow lines.

The family Fionidae includes the species *Fiona pinnata,* a 2-inch long animal that is whitish in color. It lives in groups on floating bodies in all seas; it feeds principally on *Lepas anatifera,* which is a species of barnacle.

In the family Calmidae there is only one species, *Calma glaucoides,* a tiny animal less than ½ inch long that feeds exclusively on fish eggs. The reason for this restricted diet can undoubtedly be attributed to the fact that its radula is almost totally devoid of teeth, its intestine is completely closed, and it has no anus whatsoever.

The Gymnophila

The order Gymnophila, or Soleolifera, is a small one, with only two families.

The members of the family Onchidiidae are a group of shell-less gastropods that look rather like chitons. There is a head with a pair of tentacles, each with an eye at the end. There is also a pair of oral veils at the mouth. There is a wide, flat foot and a warty mantle. The warts may contain eyes.

The terrestrial family Veronicellidae includes slugs that have no shell or mantle cavity. The bodies are flattened and elongated and the foot is greatly reduced. These slugs are generally found in tropical and subtropical zones. One species is native to the United States; this is *Veronicella floridana,* which is found in Florida.

The glassy snail Oxychilus draparnaldi, a member of the family Vitrinidae, is named for its translucent shell. The species prefers environments that are dark and humid, and it is often found in caves.

The Pulmonata

With only a few exceptions, pulmonate gastropods are at home on the land or in fresh water. In this group there may be a spiral shell, a reduced shell, or no shell. There is no operculum. Those species in which there is no shell are called slugs.

The pulmonates have lungs or lunglike organs, rather than gills. Over the course of ages the original respiratory organs of these snails—gills or ctenidia—were replaced with a sac whose walls are impregnated with blood vessels. This sac, quite properly, is described as a lung. These animals must therefore live in direct contact with the atmosphere, for they breathe air. Even those species that live primarily in water must rise to the surface periodically to replenish their supply of oxygen.

Land snails had successfully made the adaptation to a new environment from the sea by the end of the Mesozoic era. In turn, new forms that developed from them partially readapted to aquatic life. These are the freshwater snails. In returning to a watery environment, however, they retained the air-breathing respiratory system that had evolved during their ancestors' stay on land.

With rare exceptions, land snails are bound to the particular environment in which they live. That is to say, an animal accustomed to a habitat of limestone rocks will rarely be found on quartz or slate because it is thoroughly conditioned to the stony substratum with which it is familiar. A rock-dwelling snail will not be found on tree trunks; indeed, a species that prefers beeches avoids pines.

These patterns of habitat are so strongly impressed that they can be used as indicators of past geological and climatological phenomena. When the great glaciers descended on Europe during the Tertiary period, for example, only a few species of snails managed to survive, either on mountaintops or in isolated valleys that remained free of ice. When the ice retreated a million years later, other species repopulated the land. But the glacial survivors were so conditioned to their specialized environments that they remained there.

Today there are species of *Helicigona* still entrenched on high peaks in northern Italy, and species of *Clausilia* are found only on the rocky walls of certain valleys. After the glaciers receded recolonization by species peculiar to forests was delayed until natural reforestation could slowly be accomplished.

Accidental movement has played its part in diffusions of the species. Nobody knows exactly how it happened—by land, sea, or air—but in recent decades the species *Cepaea nemoralis*, native to a region near the Arctic, suddenly appeared in California. A hardy creature, it thrived in that milder climate and today has become a serious pest. Similarly, the African species *Achatina fulica* has invaded most of the Indo-Pacific area. This is a phenomenon taking place at this very moment, a phenomenon that will undoubtedly upset to a serious degree the natural equilibrium of a vast region.

Pulmonates range in size from less than $\frac{1}{10}$ inch to more than 8 inches. There is often no clear distinction between the head and body. The ventral foot, which has a sole suited for creeping, is also not distinct from the body. The foot is smooth in aquatic species but may be warty in land forms.

This subclass is divided into two orders. In the Basommatophora, which are aquatic snails, there is one pair of tentacles on the head. In the Stylommatophora, which are terrestrial snails, there are two pairs. In the first order there is an eye at the base of each tentacle; in the second, the eyes are located at the knobbed ends of the posterior pair of tentacles.

The first four superfamilies discussed below belong to the order Basommatophora, the rest belong to the Stylommatophora.

The Actophila. The superfamily Actophila includes three families of marine and terrestrial snails that have an almost worldwide distribution.

Members of the family Ellobiidae are commonly found on mudflats and in salt marshes in warmer areas. They have low-spired conical shells. A few genera are terrestrial.

The family Otinidae includes the single genus *Otina*, which is found on the rocky coasts of Great Britain. The freshwater family Chilinidae also has only one genus— *Chilina*, which is found in South America.

These animals have cup-shaped shells, which could easily cause them to be mistaken for limpets, were it not for a ridge running obliquely from the center to the right. On the inside of the shell this ridge is matched by a groove; the pulmonary sac opens into this groove. They have no tentacles.

In the family Siphonariidae, which includes the genera *Siphonaria* and *Williamia*, the members possess not only a pulmonary sac but an internal gill as well. This dual respiratory system allows them to breathe both in the air and under water. In fact, they

The land snail Delima itala, *a member of the superfamily Clausiliacea, is found in the Mediterranean area. Often seen on trees, rocks, and limestone walls, it can be identified by its long, cigar-shaped shell.*

The Amphibolacea. The superfamily Amphibolacea contains marine snails with conical shells. It includes only three genera: *Salinator*, *Amphibola*, and *Stenacme*—all members of the family Amphibolidae. All species of these genera live in brackish waters in Australia, New Zealand, and Florida, respectively.

The Siphonariacea. The superfamily Siphonariacea, also known as Patelliformia, includes limpetlike snails that inhabit rocky areas with either salt or brackish water.

live along coastlines in the littoral area between the tide limits, spending some time submerged and some time in rocks well above the water range.

Some species have a definite home to which they return after feeding. During feeding they will move only a short distance from their residence. *S. japonica*, for example, will travel only 6 inches.

The Hygrophila. The superfamily Hygrophila includes many common freshwater snails. Members of this group are found in lakes,

ponds, and streams throughout the world.

The family Trimusculidae, also called Gadiniidae, contains one genus of snails with a circular, buttonlike shell.

The pond snails belong to the families Physidae and Lymnaeidae. They form an important link in the ecological chain of freshwater lakes and streams. They feed on aquatic plants and small animals. They, in turn, form a staple in the diet of fishes, frogs, toads, and some birds.

Because pond snails have lungs, they must come to the surface of the water periodically to breathe. Most of them have the ability to creep, shell downward, on the water's surface.

These snails can be found in almost any body of fresh water. *Physa acuta* lives principally in streams; *Physa frontinalis* prefers springs and waters with a high oxygen content; *Galba truncatula* can live in a concrete-lined canal if it cannot locate its favored limestone habitat.

One of the largest members of this group is the great pond snail, *Lymnaea stagnalis,* found in still water and quiet streams from the polar circle to the Gulf of Mexico in the Western Hemisphere and to the Mediterranean in Europe. In winter this two-inch snail can sometimes be seen creeping along the underside of ice in a brook. It eats both animal and vegetable food.

The tiny *Galba truncatula,* seemingly innocuous, is indirectly and innocently one of the worst enemies of sheep and cattle, and therefore of man. As the little snail scrapes algae from the surface of ditches and ponds, embryos of *Fasciola hepatica,* a parasitic flatworm, swarm up into its shell. After developing there, the worms pass out through the snail's liver and encyst themselves on the stems of marsh grasses. Browsing sheep and cattle eat the grass, along with the encysted worms and many infested snails as well. Before long, the mammals show symptoms of the deadly disease known as rot. Worm eggs produced in the systems of the host animals are excreted with manure. In the spring, a new crop of worms renews the vicious cycle.

The family Planorbidae includes snails of worldwide distribution. Their habitats range from springs to stagnant pools to swift rivers to the stony banks of mountain lakes. They are characterized by flattened, spiral shells with a small opening. The tentacles are threadlike. Some Planorbidae carry the parasitic flukes that cause the serious disease schistosomiasis in humans.

Planorbis corneus grows to more than an inch, while *Segmentina nitida* barely reaches ¼ inch. The three-coiled orb snail, *Helisoma trivolvis,* is common throughout the United States. Its shell is yellow or brown. It is less than an inch in length.

The subfamily Bulininae includes freshwater snails with conical shells whose whorls, unlike those of most snails, run counterclockwise.

Members of the families Ancylidae and Ferrissiidae are called shield snails or freshwater limpets. They include freshwater mollusks that live attached to rocks in streams and on lake shores, and to aquatic plants in quieter waters and swamps. They have disc-shaped shells with a large opening.

The Succineacea. The superfamily Succineacea contains sluglike mollusks that live in damp places, preferably close to a stream. There is only one family—Succineidae—which has more than 25 genera and subgenera distributed throughout most of the world. These animals always choose the same kind of environment. In fact, their preference for the proximity of fresh water is so strong that they are sometimes listed as freshwater rather than terrestrial mollusks. However, they cannot live underwater.

These gastropods have delicate, thin shells with a small spire. The body whorl is comparatively large.

The Tracheopulmonata. The superfamily Tracheopulmonata includes the single family Athoracophoridae. The slugs of this group have a nonfunctional lung; they are the only mollusks in which trachea make up the respiratory apparatus. These are tree-dwelling animals that live in Australia, New Zea-

land, and the islands of the South Pacific.

The Achatinellacea. This superfamily includes the single family Achatinellidae.

The 14 genera of this group of terrestrial snails are distributed throughout the western Pacific from Japan to the Hawaiian Islands and south to Australia and New Zealand. Known as little agate shells, they range in size from about an inch to microscopic dimensions. Their conical shells are right- or left-handed, depending upon the species, and are often banded and spotted with bright colors.

In the Hawaiian Islands snails of this group lived on trees and bushes from the central watershed on each island down to sea level. Each isolated mountain valley had its own form. A catastrophe of sorts occurred in the 19th century when cattle were introduced to Hawaii. Goats had already stripped much of the undergrowth where the snails lived and the herds of cattle invaded wooded areas. As a result many species of these snails disappeared.

The Pupillacea. The superfamily Pupillacea is much larger and more widespread than the preceding superfamily. It contains more

The land snail Helix apertus *lives in the Mediterranean area. It can be recognized by the large opening in its shell and the thick white epiphragm, or "pot lid." The epiphragm closes the opening when the animal is inside.*

109

The garden snail Cepaea hortensis *(opposite page) is characterized by bright spiral bands on its shell. Found in both Europe and the United States, it usually feeds on weeds, but it will sometimes attack gardens.*

The snail Helix pomatia *(below) is the escargot made famous by French chefs. It was also a popular delicacy of the ancient Romans.*

The snail Eobania vermiculata *(bottom) is another edible species. Found in the Mediterranean area, it has an attractive banded shell.*

than 100 genera distributed throughout most of the world. The snails of this superfamily have shells of a conical-cylindrical shape, and are quite tiny. In the Hawaiian branch of this large family there are some snails that bear their young alive, a rarity among terrestrial pulmonates.

Among the interesting species is *Chondrina avenacea.* These snails gather in large colonies wherever there are calcareous rocks. *Gastrocopta armifera* is an animal with a black, thimble-shaped shell ⅓ inch tall; it inhabits damp soil and the undersides of logs in the eastern half of the United States.

The family Vertiginidae includes widely distributed small snails with cylindrical shells. The shell opening is small and has teeth. In the members of this group the anterior pair of tentacles are either small or absent.

Snails of the family Valloniidae have small shells that are generally rounded. They may be flattened or have a low spire. This family includes the genus *Vallonia. V. pulchella* is common in the northern United States and Canada. It is found in damp, dark places. It is a small animal, only ⅛

inch in diameter. Its thin, light-colored shell is transparent. *V. costata* is another small species. Its shell is gray and has ribs.

Vallonia pulchella deserves mention because it can be found almost anywhere in the Northern Hemisphere, and has extended its range to the Equator. A scant ⅛ inch in diameter, it always hides from the light under tree bark, moss, or fragments of rock. The transparency of its shell and its small size render it almost invisible.

Truncatella californica, the California looping snail, is another midget member worth looking for. An amphibious snail, it hides among seaweeds or stones on the beach, or in brackish meadows on grass stems. When it moves, it loops along like an inchworm, using both foot and snout for locomotion.

The family Megaspiridae includes *Megaspira elatior,* a forest snail of South America. Its auger-shaped shell, with about 25 coils, is more than 2 inches long.

The family Clausiliidae is widely distributed in the mountains of Europe and Asia. Some are also found in Africa and South America. This group is characterized by the presence of a *clausilium,* a shelly plate that closes over the opening like a door whenever the animal withdraws into its shell. The clausilium, which is attached to the columella, probably protects the animal from loss of water. The opening in this family is usually pear-shaped and furrowed with ridges.

Commonly found genera include *Clausilia, Laciniaria,* and *Balea.* The tree-dwelling *Balea perversa* is the only Old World clausiliid without a clausilium.

The family Cochlicopidae contains small gastropods with elongated, conical shells. The shell opening, which has no teeth, may be round or elongated. There are about 200 species in this group. *Cochlicopa lubrica,* which is found both in Europe and North America, has a yellowish shell about ⅕ inch

On these pages we see various gastropod, or snail, shells. The locale and superfamily (in parenthesis) of each species is given:

On these pages we see various gastropod, or snail, shells. The locale and superfamily (in parenthesis) of each species is given:

1. *Newcombia plicata from Hawaii (superfamily Achatinellidae)*
2. *Partulina variabilis from Hawaii (Achatinellidae)*
3. *Amastra magna from Hawaii (Amastridae)*
4 and 5. *Ryssota maxima from the Philippines (Helicarionidae)*
6. *Achatina fulica from central Africa (Achatinidae)*

high. It lives in humid places, such as under piles of dead leaves.

The large family Enidae is widely represented in Eurasia and Africa. Members of this group have moderate-sized conical shells. Common genera are *Ena* and *Zebrina*.

The Achatinacea. The superfamily Achatinacea is represented by many genera, most of which are common throughout the world. Shells of this group are known as agate shells. They are oval or cigar-shaped and sometimes turreted. Although they are found throughout the world, they thrive best in tropical regions. Among the members are

genera as small as ⅕ inch in diameter, such as *Cecilioides*. At the other extreme is the largest of the terrestrial gastropods, *Achatina achatina*, which reaches 9 inches in length. This species is native to central Africa. This large agate shell lays eggs that are over an inch long.

Achatina fulica has expanded its range in the past 200 years and particularly since World War II, when it was carried from Southeast Asia to most of the islands of the Pacific.

A major problem with these snails is the rapid rate at which they multiply and become serious pests in their new environments.

le: in Southeast
_, their natural
and keep the popula-
new environments their
_w. However, the rate of their
ex_ _vas slowed after their initial in-
vasion _ various bacterial diseases and by
other predatory snails.

In Europe, the tiny *Cecilioides acicula*
is common but difficult to find alive, since
it lives in microfissures in the ground.
Rumina decollata inhabits the entire Mediterranean area, living under stones in brush-
covered regions. The young in this species
are cigar-shaped and have all the turns of

their shells intact. But as they grow the
early whorls break off; by the time they reach
maturity they are left with only about two-
thirds of a shell.

Another interesting species is *Achatina
panthera*, the panther agate shell of Mozam-
bique and the South African coast. Striped
and tawny like its namesake, it lives in hollows in rocks and trees, out of the sun.
During dry seasons these snails, a dozen or
more in a group, will go into a state of semi-
hibernation in their hollow, sealing the openings in their shells with an *epiphragm*, a
covering of calcified slime, to prevent dry-
ing out.

7. Achatina variegata
   *from Africa (Achatini-
   dae)*
8. Strophocheilus pope-
   lairianus *from South
   America (Acavidae)*
9. Ampelita xystera
   *from Madagascar
   (Acaviade)*
10. Xenothauma baroni
    *from Peru (Bulimuli-
    dae)*
11. Dryptus moritzianus
    *from Venezuela (Buli-
    mulidae)*
12. Placostylus fibratus
    bovinus *from New
    Caledonia (Bulimuli-
    dae)*

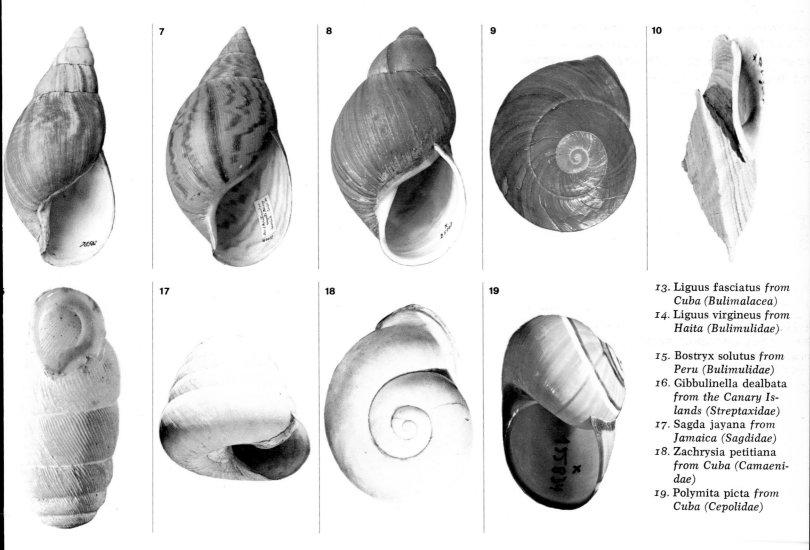

13. Liguus fasciatus *from
    Cuba (Bulimalacea)*
14. Liguus virgineus *from
    Haita (Bulimulidae)*

15. Bostryx solutus *from
    Peru (Bulimulidae)*
16. Gibbulinella dealbata
    *from the Canary Is-
    lands (Streptaxidae)*
17. Sagda jayana *from
    Jamaica (Sagdidae)*
18. Zachrysia petitiana
    *from Cuba (Camaeni-
    dae)*
19. Polymita picta *from
    Cuba (Cepolidae)*

The Oleacinacea. The superfamily Oleacinacea includes some of the largest and most interesting snails. There are two families in this group—Testacellidae and Oleacinidae. Snails of these families are all carnivorous; they generally prey on other mollusks.

Members of the family Testacellidae live predominantly in the tropics of Central and South America. They have a minute, ear-shaped shell found at the posterior end of the slug-like, elongated body. Rapacious hunters, they slide their long bodies into the burrows of their victims and seize them with the radula. This organ is armed with back-slanted teeth, so the harder the victim struggles the more firmly it impales itself. The snail usually swallows its prey whole, its stomach stretching to accommodate a large meal.

Testacella is the only genus of this family. Its members are usually active at night. They also emerge in wet weather because they don't like heavily saturated earth. In dry weather, on the other hand, they dig several feet underground to find the proper amount of moisture; sometimes they seal the body in a waxy coat of mucus to stem evaporation. Years ago, before the soil-building value of earthworms was appreciated, gardeners used *Testacella* to rid their plots of the worms, which they thought were pests.

Members of the family Oleacinidae have a large shell with a narrow opening. The body is long and narrow. Even the great snails of the family Bulimulidae are no match for these killers. With a radula as wickedly armed as that of *Testacella*, an oleacinid forces its way into a closed snail shell and drags its victim out. Sometimes this cannibal will bore through the shell of a victim and suck out the soft parts.

Euglandina rosea, resident of the southeastern United States, averages about 2 inches in length and has a rosy yellow shell. *Natalina cafra* is a 4-inch, flesh-eating snail from South Africa.

The Endodontacea. The superfamily Endodontacea includes gastropods with small shells. The two families in this group—Arionidae and Endodontidae—have a very wide distribution.

The family Endodontidae includes snails with conical or flattened shells, which are often ribbed or lined with brown markings.

Punctum minutissimum is a mollusk that loves moist places. It is found under clumps of moss, stones, and in beds of rotting leaves, particularly near brooks and ponds. *Discus rotundatus*, a somewhat larger relative with a disc-shaped shell ornamented by reddish markings, enjoys the same habitat.

Members of the genus *Anguispira* have relatively large shells with spires. They are often ribbed or striated. *A. kochi* has a white or reddish shell with brown bands. It is about 1 inch in diameter. *A. alternata* has a yellow shell with reddish-brown blotches. It is com-

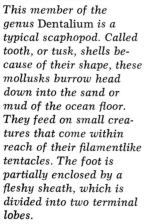

This member of the genus Dentalium *is a typical scaphopod. Called tooth, or tusk, shells because of their shape, these mollusks burrow head down into the sand or mud of the ocean floor. They feed on small creatures that come within reach of their filamentlike tentacles. The foot is partially enclosed by a fleshy sheath, which is divided into two terminal lobes.*

mon in damp places, such as rotting logs; several of these animals may be found together.

The slugs of the family Arionidae have a very small shell that is covered by the mantle. *Arion ater* is a large slug, sometimes 6 inches long. Its shell is little more than a few calcareous granules under the mantle. Its color ranges from pale orange to black. Common in central Europe and now spreading to bordering countries, it causes great damage to crops. A voracious eater, this animal has a remarkably undiscriminating palate. One captive specimen was reported to have consumed, with apparently equal relish, five other slugs, a dead mussel, insects, a scrap of soap, dead mice, birds, earthworms, bread, wild plants, poisonous mushrooms, fern leaves, sea holly, a piece of newspaper, and a handful of beach sand!

Arion is primarily an Old World genus. Species of the genus *Ariolimax* are common in the United States in the states bordering the Pacific. *A. columbianus* is yellowish or greenish and may be up to 6 inches long. It inhabits damp forests. *A. niger*, which is gray or black, is only about 2 inches long.

If necessary, slugs can go without eating for days at a time. But they must have water or they will die. Many species can remain underwater for long periods of time, even days, with no apparent ill effects. The slime they secrete, and on which they glide, both lubricates and protects their bodies. If a slug's path is blocked by a sharp knife or razor, the slug will go up and over the edge without suffering a nick.

The Zonitacea. The superfamily Zonitacea includes a large number of genera found from the tropics all the way north to the Arctic. Their shells are generally translucent and disc-shaped, and sometimes so small as to be insignificant.

The slugs of the family Limacidae are chiefly herbivorous mollusks that creep about in woods and gardens after rains and at dusk, when dew begins to form. Sometimes they suspend themselves from bushes by glutinous threads. The shell is a thin plate that is covered by the mantle.

Limax maximus is the largest member of its genus and one of the largest members of the family. Its 5- to 6-inch body is gray or pale brown, and alternately striped and dotted with black. Originally a European species, it was introduced into the United States during the 19th century by gardeners trained in Europe. Strangely enough, for a member of a vegetable-eating clan, this slug reportedly ate worms and meat, snails, and other slugs, all kinds of food scraps, and even the bindings from old books. But it would not touch the green of growing plants. It was therefore extolled as the gardener's friend.

Its relative, *Deroceras reticulatum*, on the other hand, is considered one of the worst garden and farm pests. It comes out at night and devours everything that grows, from tender seedlings to succulent, ripening fruits.

Members of the family Vitrinidae, known as the glassy shells because of the translucence of their small coverings, are nocturnal creatures who prefer humid places out of reach of the sun. They range into the Arctic and sometimes can be seen gliding along on the surface of snow. *Oxychilus cellarius*, a typical species, is omnivorous and quite capable of killing and eating butterflies.

This drawing shows the anatomy of a scaphopod. The labeled parts are:
1. *captaculi—small, beadlike swellings on the ends of the tentacles*
2. *mouth*
3. *nervous system*
4. *esophagus*
5. *kidney*
6. *epatopancreas*
7. *reproductive organ*
8. *posterior opening of mantle*
9. *shell*
10. *pallial nerve*
11. *anus*
12. *intestine*
13. *mantle*
14. *foot*

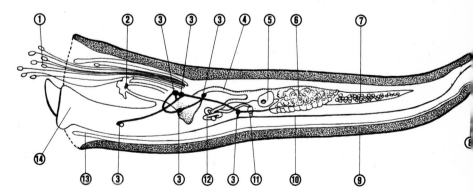

The Zonitidae, numerous in Europe and North America, show cannibalistic tendencies when first hatched—a strong, hungry specimen will eat its weaker brothers, shell and all. These lovers of dark, damp places give off a strange onion odor, which probably suggests a taste disagreeable to their natural enemies—birds, frogs, and toads.

The family Polygyridae includes only a few genera of land snails found in North America and the West Indies. One species, *Triodopsis albolabris,* is familiar to all hikers and campers in the eastern United States. Known as the white-lipped snail, this gastropod has a yellowish shell composed of many whorls; the thick white lip of the shell is flanged. Its long, slender, and mottled body carries four "horns," the longest bearing black eyes. These 1-inch snails live under rotting leaves and decaying logs.

Most species of this family have many teeth at the opening of the shell; one of the most richly equipped is *Polygyra auriculata* of Florida. Most also have disc-shaped shells, but two species from Jamaica, *Lacteoluna turbiniformis* and *Sagda jayana,* have shells in the form of high cones.

The Acavacea. The snails of the superfamily Acavacea, ranking with the largest on land, are diffused widely through South America, South Africa, Madagascar, Ceylon, and Australia. Shell shapes vary; they can be elongated or disclike.

Strophocheilus ovatus from the forests of South America is one of the largest of the land snails, reaching a length of 6 inches. Its eggs are white, hard-shelled, and the size of pigeon eggs. The snail lays them, a few at a time, in a ground nest covered with dead leaves.

The Bulimulacea. These snails live mainly in North, Central, and South America. Some are found in Australia and nearby islands. They generally have conical shells with spires varying from low to high. Some, however, such as *Xenothauma baroni,* are closer in appearance to the disc shape of the Helicidae. Many of the smaller species of bulimulids are gaily colored and have curious lip expansions.

Among the largest members of the family are *Placostylus fibratus bovinus,* a New Caledonia species that exceeds 5 inches, and *Dryptus moritzianus,* a Venezuelan species that reaches 4½ inches.

Members of the genus *Liguus* are smaller. They have strikingly colored shells. Species are found in southern Florida, Hispaniola, and Cuba. These include *L. virgineus, L. vittatus,* and *L. fasciatus.* Some of these snails are pure white; others have bands of pink, olive, lavender, yellow, and black in varying widths. Some are beautifully pinstriped with pale green on white.

Species of the genus *Bulimulus* have shells that are usually of a dull color, and most are solid rather than striped. *B. dealbatus* is found in the southern United States. It has a thin, white shell with gray lines; the shell opening is oval. It is less than an inch in length.

To hibernate in winter, these animals attach their shells to the bark of a tree with a gluelike secretion. Try to pry one loose, and the bark may break off before the cement gives way. In this state, many of the snails are opened and eaten by tree crabs.

The Streptaxacea. The superfamily Streptaxacea includes about 60 genera. Their only representatives in Europe are fossil species from the Cretaceous period. However, they are quite widely distributed elsewhere.

These are all carnivorous and predatory snails, preying primarily on other mollusks. Their shells, generally fragile, are in the form of a depressed disc. Species of the genus *Chlamydephorus,* found in South Africa, are unusual in that the very small shell is covered by the mantle.

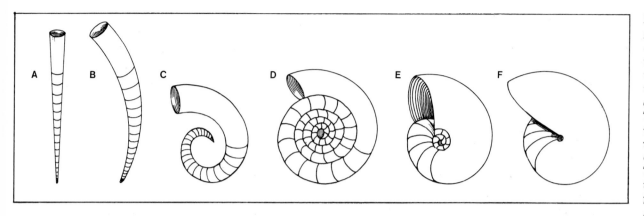

Too attractive a shell can be the undoing of a snail, especially when the collectors turn out in force. Shell seekers in New Zealand have been hunting so eagerly and successfully for specimens of the genus *Paryphanta* that the government has had to ban exportation of the shells.

The Helicacea. The superfamily Helicacea is the largest group of land snails, including more than 180 genera. Its best-known member is the edible snail, *Helix pomatia*. This snail has been considered a food delicacy since the times of the ancient Romans.

Distributed throughout the world and truly cosmopolitan, the Helicacea can be found in tropical jungles, in the coniferous forests of Scandinavia, in North American deserts, on the rocky slopes of the Alps, and in the mild regions around the Mediterranean to which they are native. The shell in this highly evolved group is generally broad and conical with a low spire. The surface is often wrinkled.

The dimensions of the several thousand species of Helicacea vary considerably. In Cuba, for example, there are specimens of *Zachrysia petitiana* with shells that reach almost 3 inches in diameter. On the other end of the scale is the little *Drepanostoma nautiliforme*, peculiar to a number of valleys in the Italian provinces of Varese and Como,

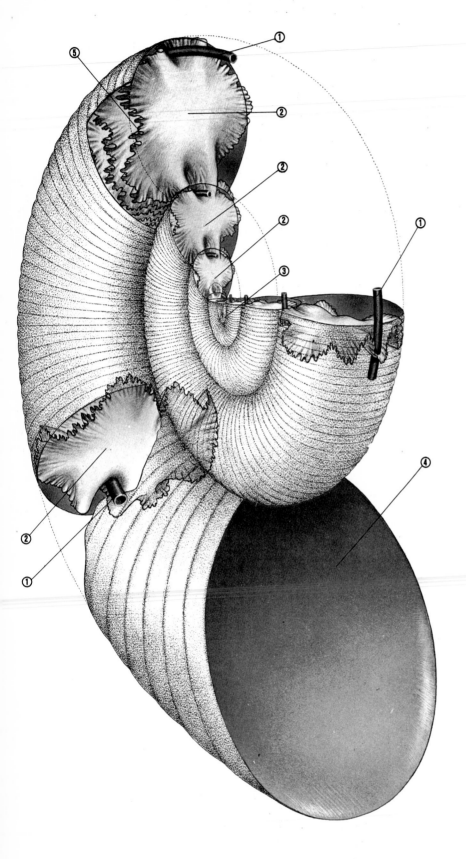

which barely achieves a length of ⅕ inch.

Regardless of size, many genera have an unusual feature in their genital apparatus; this is an organ, the dart sac, capable of producing small calcareous darts, which the animals thrust into each other's muscles during copulation.

Many species have strikingly colored shells, the largest and most beautiful, as is usual, belonging to the tropical species. Foremost among these are some members of the genus *Papuina*, found in New Guinea, and the genus *Polymita* of Cuba. There are also showy forms in the Philippines, Mauritius, and the West Indies. United States' species are, for the most part, dull in color and small in size.

Members of the Helicidae can be found almost everywhere throughout the Mediterranean region. The most familiar species are *Cernuella virgata*, *Leucochroa cespitum*, and *Cochlicella acuta*. A characteristic species is *Theba pisana*, which lives in hot, dry places, but always reasonably near the sea. These snails live in large colonies on low-branched trees and shrubs.

The genus *Helix* includes hundreds of species, mostly limited to Europe. *Helix pomatia* is about 2 inches long and has a thin, yellowish-brown shell that is often banded. *H. aspersa* is yellow or gray with brown bands. The body whorl and the shell opening are both large. This snail is less than an inch in diameter.

Like *Helix*, *Cepaea* is a native European genus. *C. hortensis* has a yellow shell with dark bands and is about ½ inch high. *C. nemoralis* is probably the most familiar member of the helices in northern and central Europe. Individuals of this species vary in size and in the number of bands decorating the shell. Some are ½ to ¾ inch in diameter while others range up to 1½ inches. Smaller species have up to five bands; the larger species seem to have no fixed limit to the number of bands.

Tusk Shells— Scaphopoda

The tusk, or tooth, shells of the class Scaphopoda are shaped like an elephant's tusk and are often white or ivory in color. This group includes about 350 species of burrowing marine mollusks.

The first fossil records of this group are from the Devonian period, about 400 million years ago. However, scaphopods were most numerous and showed their greatest diversity of form during the Cretaceous period. After that, most became extinct.

Scaphopods are found in all seas, ranging from the shallows to depths of more than 2,600 fathoms. Their elongated bodies vary in size from slender 1-inch, hollow needles to tapered 5-inch tubes.

Anatomy. The scaphopod shell is open at both ends. The foot extends from the larger opening, which is the anterior end of the animal. There is no true head. The mouth opens on the end of a short snout, or proboscis, just above the foot at the anterior end. Clustered around the mouth are a series of threadlike tentacles, each of which is tipped by a tiny, beadlike swelling. These structures are called *captacula*. They extend out into the surrounding sand; the adhesive knobs at the tips are used to capture prey.

Burrowing with its foot into a sandy bottom, which it prefers, or into mud, the tusk shell stands in a slanting position. Its anterior end is buried and its narrower, posterior end projects up into clear water. Water enters and leaves the animal through the posterior opening.

This constant flow of water supplies the animal with food and oxygen. Scaphopods have no gills; the respiratory exchange takes place over the surface of the mantle. The long, thin tentacles around the mouth stretch out in all directions in the sand ready to seize the microscopic organisms on which the Scaphopoda feed.

The mouth contains a radula with large, flat teeth; it is used to take in the prey from the captacula. The digestive system consists of a short esophagus, a stomach, a digestive gland, and an intestine that loops back to discharge through the anus into the mantle cavity near the foot.

The circulatory system is rudimentary, consisting of a number of blood sinuses. There is no heart. The nervous system consists of several ganglia and their associated nerve cords. Sense organs, including eyes, tentacles, and osphradia are absent.

The sexes are separate. Fertilization is external. Sperm and eggs reach the outside through one of the kidneys, which are connected to a nephridiopore opening near the anus. The larvae are of the trochophore type.

One of the unusual features of scaphopods is the presence, in the embryonic stage, of small bivalve shells that become welded together as the animal grows. However, other characteristics—the presence of a radula, the form of the visceral sac, and the unpaired gonad—indicate that scaphopods are close relatives of the gastropods.

Classification. The class Scaphopoda is divided into two families. The larger of the two is the Dentaliidae, which contains the largest and most numerous species. The foot in this family is conical, pointed, and partially enclosed by a fleshy sheath that is split into two side lobes. The radula has a large central tooth flanked by lateral and marginal teeth.

The most common species of the single genus of the Dentaliidae, at least on both coasts of the Atlantic, is *Dentalium entale*, the common tooth shell. This ivory-white shell is 2 inches long and slightly curved.

In the warmer European waters *D. dentalis* is well known, as is *D. vulgare*. This

Ammonites (opposite page) became extinct about 65 million years ago. This diagram shows the structure of an ammonite shell. The labeled parts are:
1. *siphuncle*
2. *walls of the fragmocone*
3. *embryonic chamber*
4. *living chamber*
5. *lobal, or suture, line*

latter shell, a lusterless white with a tinge of rose or yellow toward the apex, averages less than 2 inches in length except on the Adriatic shores, where fine specimens surpassing the 2-inch mark have been collected.

Several attractive Dentaliidae inhabit the waters of the Far East. These include the largest of the scaphopods. *Dentalium elephantinum,* which ranges up to 5 inches in length. Usually dark green fading to white at the apex, these handsome shells are found near Japan and the Philippines. Another striking specimen from Philippine waters is the glossy pea-green *Dentalium aprinum,* a slender, gracefully curving shell between 2 and 3 inches long.

The scaphopod with the most interesting history is probably *Dentalium pretiosum,* the money tooth shell of the Pacific coast north of California. A little over an inch in length, white and polished and perforated by nature as if intended for stringing, these shells were converted by the Indians into necklaces and *haik-wa,* a form of wampum.

In the family Siphonodentaliidae the shell is more cylindrical than tusklike, quite small, and may have a notch in the smaller end. The foot is long and contractile; its end can expand to form a terminal sucker. There are three genera in the family, distinguished by the form of their shells.

Octopuses, Squids, and Others— Cephalopoda

Judging by external appearances, only a zoologist would recognize a relationship between snails, clams, and chitons, and the highly organized cephalopods. The animals in this class—octopuses, squids, cuttlefish, argonauts, and nautiluses—are among the most agile and ferocious creatures in the sea. Exclusively marine, they can be found in all the oceans of the world, from the Arctic to the Antarctic, from the shallows to the abyssal depths. They are the largest and most specialized of the mollusks.

The name Cephalopoda is the key to the anatomy of this class. It comes from two Greek words, *cephalos,* meaning "head," and *podos,* meaning "foot." Literally, then, the name means "head-footed animal." This refers to the fact that the foot in these mollusks has been divided into arms, which surround the head and siphon inside the mantle cavity. This combined head and foot is called the cephalopodium. The rest of the body, with its visceral organs, extends behind the

The photo of a delicately-patterned ammonite fossil (below left), shows clearly the highly indented suture lines.

The drawing (below right) shows various types of suture lines, which mark the division between the walls on the inside of the shell and the fragmocone.
A. goniatitic suture
B. ceratitic suture
C and D. two types of ammonitic sutures

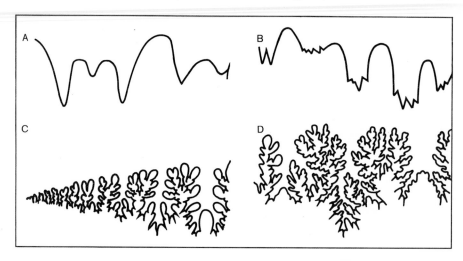

cephalopodium. In the squids, this body extension is pointed or cigar shaped; in the octopuses, it is like a bulbous pouch.

Only the nautiluses of the South Pacific and the female argonaut retain a visible shell. One species of the spirula, or ram's horn, *Spirula spirula*, has a spiral shell embedded at the end of the body. The squids have long internal shells of a horny or calcareous substance buried in the body covering. The cuttlefish have a flat internal *cuttlebone* of calcareous material. In the octopuses there is no trace of a shell at all.

The cephalopod body is protected by the thick, muscular wall of the mantle. In the mantle cavity are the gills, the anus, and the openings for the genital organs. Water drawn in through the open edge of the mantle above the neck is forced out through the siphon, or funnel, on the lower side by contractions of the powerful mantle muscles.

The squids and cuttlefish are especially well equipped for high-speed swimming. A jet of water expelled from a funnel extended forward shoots the animal backwards like a torpedo. By bending the funnel to the rear, the animal can dart forward quickly to seize its prey. In addition, many squids are equipped with "fins," a pair of triangular folds at the dorsal end of the mantle, which can be undulated to assist movement and which are of great assistance in changing direction.

Almost everybody thinks of a writhing mass of tentacles when he visualizes the cephalopods. This is actually true only of the nautiluses, which have about 90 tentacles. In the octopuses there are 8 appendages, which are properly called arms rather than tentacles. In the squids and cuttlefish—the decapods—there are 8 arms and 2 tentacles. The tentacles are longer than the arms and are used to seize prey. They can be retracted into the body.

Cephalopods are carnivorous, preying on fish and many invertebrates, including crus-

taceans and snails. In most cephalopods, the mouth is circular and armed with a horny, parrotlike beak; this beak is a formidable weapon worked by powerful muscles. Behind it is the linguinal ribbon with a typical molluscan radula. The long, narrow esophagus leads to a stomach with fleshy walls. The stomach is followed by the intestine, which opens through a pore in the mantle cavity. Wastes are expelled through the funnel. A special ink sac also opens into the funnel.

All cephalopods except the nautiluses have two gills, two kidneys, and three hearts. Two hearts pump deoxygenated blood through the gills; the other pumps oxygenated blood to the rest of the body. The nervous system is highly developed; the brain is large, and the eyes in all but the nautilus have a structure similar to that of vertebrate eyes. These animals also have a sense of smell. The sexes are separate, and the males have one or more special organs for copulating.

There are two subclasses of Cephalopoda —the Tetrabranchiata and the Dibranchiata. The Tetrabranchia have two pairs of gills and an external shell. This group includes only the members of the genus *Nautilus*. The Dibranchia includes all other living cephalopods. These mollusks have one pair of gills and there may be either an internal shell or no shell.

An impression in the rock (above left) was made by plates on the shell of the ammonite Laevaptychus longus. *These plates, or aptychi, served as a trapdoor to close the entrance to the ammonite shell.*

Ammonites of the genus Placenticeras *(above right) lived during the Upper Cretaceous, some 80 million years ago. This fossilized shell shows tooth marks left by a mosasaur, a marine reptile that lived during the same epoch.*

Cephalopods of the Past

There are many more extinct forms of cephalopods than there are living. Some 10,000 fossil species are known; today, less than 1,000 species exist. The earliest members of this class were the nautiloids, followed by the ammonoids and the belemnoids.

The Nautiloidea. The most ancient of the cephalopods, the nautiloids first appeared during the Cambrian period, between 600 and 500 million years ago. From fossil evidence, it is thought that this group once consisted of about 2,500 species. They are represented today only by five species of the genus *Nautilus*, which are diffused along the western margins of the Pacific Ocean. However, it is not reasonable to assume that these last living representatives of this group have survived unchanged. Enormous evolutionary alterations have occurred during that huge span of time, changing the form of the shell, the internal anatomy, and, even more important, the habits and mode of life.

Nautiloids may be divided into three subclasses—Endoceratoidea, Actinoceratoidea, and Nautiloidea. These differ from each other in external appearance as well as in the internal structure of the shell.

The Endoceratoidea, consisting of forms that lived in the span of time between the Lower Ordorcian and Upper Silurian, were characterized by a straight shell and by a *siphuncle*, a membranous extension of the body formed like a length of hose.

The Actinoceratoidea had a straight or slightly bent shell, a wide siphuncle with extensive restrictions at regular intervals, and a system of secondary siphuncles.

In the subclass Nautiloidea, shells varied from straight to highly curved. A thin siphuncle maintained a constant diameter for the entire length of the shell.

The order Ellesmerocerida are a small group now placed in the subclass Nautiloidea. They are very important because they are considered to be the ancestors of the other groups. They are thought to have given rise to the Endoceratoidea during the Lower Ordovician and to the Actinoceratoidea during the Middle Ordovician. These two groups evolved in parallel development during the Paleozoic era until the former became extinct during the Middle Silurian. The second group lived much longer, not becoming extinct until the Upper Carboniferous.

The evolutionary line of the Nautiloidea started between the Lower and Middle Silurian with the development of the orders Orthocerida (which became extinct in the Upper Triassic), Ascocerida and Tarphycerida (which lived until the end of the Silurian), Discocorida and Barrandeocerida (which became extinct in the Devonian), and Oncocerida. This latter order became extinct during the Carboniferous period, but only after having given rise to the Nautilida, which survived through the Mesozoic, Cenozoic, and Quarternary periods and has come down to the present.

The most obvious common characteristic of these groups was the presence of an external shell divided internally into numerous chambers traversed by the long siphuncle. The chambers were filled with gas, which by means of density variations determined by the siphuncle, enabled the animal to move up and down in the water.

In general terms, the shell of a nautiloid was divided into two principal parts, the *fragmocone* and the *living chamber*. There was also an embryonic cup. The fragmocone, the long part, was divided into numerous chambers by walls perpendicular to the longitudinal axis of the shell. The walls, or septa, had holes for the passage of the siphuncle. The living chamber, closed at the rear by the last wall, had an opening that differed widely in the various groups. A classic example was the T-shaped opening

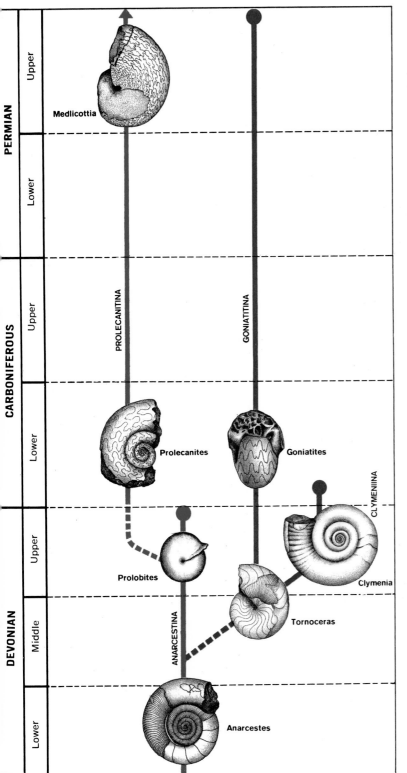

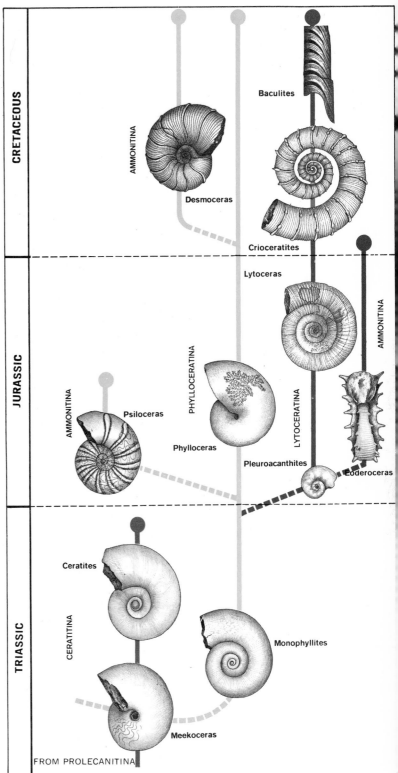

of some nautiloids of the Silurian and Carboniferous periods.

The external surface of the shell was formed by two distinct layers. The outer one was porcelaneous while the inner one was mother-of-pearl; both, however, consisted of thin plates of conchiolin and aragonite. The outer surface had ornamentation ranging from simple growth lines to parallel ribs and grooves.

The largest nautiloids were the 15-feet-long members of the genus *Endoceras*.

The Ammonoidea. Approximately 400 million years ago, toward the end of the Paleozoic era, there appeared in the seas the first ammonites. Their arrival so long ago, and their abrupt extinction, pose one of the most discussed problems of modern paleontology. The ammonites lived on earth for some 350 million years, from the beginning of the De-

Crioceratites was a common ammonite of the Lower Cretaceous epoch. Its shell is curled into a spiral, but the individual turns do not come into contact with each other.

vonian to the end of the Cretaceous period. During that lengthy period they enjoyed an abundance that was almost prodigious. At their high point, there were probably about 600 genera of ammonites. The largest species of the group, *Pachydiscus septemarodensis*, was 6 feet in diameter. Then, about 60 million years ago, they died out completely and abruptly, leaving only their resistant outer shells as evidence of their existence.

Because their soft parts were not preserved, even in those extremely fine sediments that saved far more fragile and perishable structures, the true form of the ammonite body is not known. Only the close similarities between the fossil shells of these creatures and the well-known shells of living nautiluses have enabled scientists to make some comparisons between the two groups of animals.

Through these comparisons, ammonites have been classified as cephalopods with a spiraled external shell that can be considered the result of the curling up in a plane of an elongated cone. This shell, like that of the nautilus, consisted of three parts: the embryonic cup; the fragmocone, a long, compartmented structure; and the living chamber, open toward the outside, in which the animal was housed.

While the nautiloid shell has simple sculpturing, the ammonite shell was heavily sculptured. In the nautiloids, the inner septa attached to the outer walls of the shell were only slightly curved, and their points of attachment—the *sutures*—were straight. In the ammonites the septa were intricately folded and wrinkled and their sutures were highly complex. The pattern of the suture lines is used for classification of these groups.

The fragmocone is the most interesting part of the shell structure, primarily because its solid construction has made it the best preserved segment of the shell. As in the nautiloids it consists of numerous chambers formed by interior walls arranged perpendicularly to the external walls of the shell. When the animal was alive, these chambers were filled with a mixture of gases. Changing the density of these gases enabled the ammonite to alter its weight. Like a submarine, it could make itself heavier to descend in the ocean, or lighter to rise toward the surface. The living chamber, actually the last compartment of the fragmocone, varied from one species to another, generally from a half-turn of the shell to a turn and a half. It contained the soft parts—the true body of the animal. The body was attached to the first wall by means of a membranous organ—the siphuncle—which was impregnated with calcium carbonate. This was a tube that originated in the posterior part of the body and passed through a hole in each of the septa until it reached the embryonic cup. There it ended in a blind bulb, the *caecum,* which was attached to the walls of the chamber by a calcareous cord known as the *prosiphuncle.* The siphuncle probably had the function of regulating the density of the gaseous mixture filling the chambers of the fragmocone, although we do not know exactly how it functioned.

The living chamber was large enough for the animal to withdraw into completely. Once inside, the opening could be sealed off by means of an operculum, known as the *aptychus,* consisting of one or two probably horny pieces carried by the lower portion of the mantle and ornamented in a variety of ways. The lip of the opening also varied greatly in form—sometimes smooth, sometimes twisted, sometimes equipped with a beak or with lateral hollows.

The growth of the animal took place in steps. As the animal grew, its mantle slowly built a new wall, at the same time enlarging the shell at the side of the opening in a continuous and uniform manner. When the wall was completed, the animal moved forward into its new living quarters. The time required to add a complete turn of the spiral to the shell probably ranged from four months to three years.

From the complex structure of the ammonite shell we can tell that these cephalopod mollusks were adapted to an open sea environment and included types that could float in the water, which possibly explains the far-reaching distribution of the group. However, the shells of dead animals could be transported by the ocean currents over considerable distances, which may explain why ammonite fossils are found in rocks deposited in the most diverse environments.

The ammonites evolved from the Nautiloidea during the Lower Devonian. We do not know, however, the intermediate forms between these two groups of cephalopods, with the possible exception of the bactritids. These organisms of uncertain affinity had internal characteristics analagous to those of the ammonites and a straight shell similar to that of the primitive nautiloids. Using this problematical group as a base, some scholars have put forward the theory that ammonites were derived from the Nautiloidea during the Silurian. However, since the first ammonites had flat, spiral shells, other scientists believe that later, spiral-shelled nautiloids were the ancestors of this group.

From their first appearance in the Devonian, the ammonites began to displace their contemporary nautiloids. The ammonites developed slowly throughout the Paleozoic. Their forms were not abundant, but there were four suborders, originating types very different from each other and laying the groundwork for subsequent development and proliferation of the order. In fact, in subsequent periods, once the basic type had been fixed, just a few principal groups emerged; but each group was extremely rich in forms similar to each other.

The first to appear were the representatives of the suborder Anarcestina, which lived during the Devonian period and became extinct before the beginning of the Carboniferous. From them, during the Middle Devonian, came the suborder Clymeniina, extinct by the end of the Upper Devonian. At this time the suborder Prolecanitina developed, important because some of its members were progenitors of the Mesozoic ammonites during the Triassic period. The Goniatitina, more abundant in varieties than the others, originated during the Middle Devonian from the primitive genus *Anarcestina*, and eventually died off at the end of the Permian period.

A first evolutional explosion, in the true sense of the phrase, occurred at the beginning of the Triassic, with the development of two further orders with a large number of species. Indeed, at this time the ammonites began to assert themselves in a prelude to the fantastic development they were to undergo during the next two geologic periods. Two additional suborders appeared at the beginning of the Jurassic. One of these was the immense Ammonitina, which had as many as 63 families and lasted until the Cretaceous period.

Discussion of the Mesozoic ammonites becomes complex. The enormous variety of forms makes it almost impossible to recognize the principal roads followed by evolution. During the transition between the Paleozoic era and the Triassic period, the Prolecanitina gave rise to the Ceratitina, a suborder containing the most primitive Mesozoic ammonites. These animals became extinct at the end of the Triassic, but only after giving birth to the Phylloceratina, a suborder that continued to grow throughout the Mesozoic, and gave rise during the Upper Triassic to the mollusks of the suborder Lytoceratina.

Greater problems are encountered in the study of the last and largest of the groups, the Ammonitina, a suborder including the greater part of all the Mesozoic types. This suborder is not very homogeneous, and may have had several different origins. A first group, with forms found only in the Lower Jurassic, seems to have been derived from the Phylloceratina. A second seems to have come from the same source, but during the Lower Cretaceous. And a last group apparently evolved from the Lytoceratina during the Lower Jurassic.

Toward the beginning of the Cretaceous period there began to appear in the known suborders groups of degenerate ammonites —animals with shells tending toward a second spiral, and even some straight forms. This was the final phase in the evolutional history of the ammonites. Accentuation of certain characteristics led to extremely specialized forms, which were unable to adapt to environmental changes. Life became difficult; each small environmental change became lethal. Some evolved into more primitive forms, but this led to even greater complications and also to extinction.

The great abundance of forms, however, poses another question: What caused this great variety?

It may be that ammonites appeared at a particularly favorable moment in the history of our planet. Their primitive structure, not yet specialized, permitted adaptation to the most adverse conditions, and the ammonites adapted with an amazing plasticity that made them masters of the seas in their period. Their structure, more functional than that of nautiloids, enabled them to ascend a higher rung of the evolutional ladder. But the same structure, developed to excess, became a burden that led the group to early extinction within a comparatively brief time.

The ammonites have great value in paleontology as guide fossils, which is how scientists refer to species that lived in a large geographical area but only for a brief period in the geological past. Guide fossils enable geologists to date layers of rock deposited during various geological eras—not in millions of years, but in comparative age.

Fossil remains of a species that rose and fell rapidly leave a time mark on rock layers; if we know when the animal thrived, we know when the rock was formed. Obviously, species which remained unchanged for long periods of time are useless for this purpose.

The Belemnoidea. All living cephalopods except members of the genus *Nautilus* are thought to have arisen from a now-extinct group known as the belemnoids. These primitive mollusks arose during the Triassic period, some 200 million years ago. By the end of the Cretaceous period, 65 million years ago, they have almost completely disappeared.

Like many modern cephalopods, belemnoids had an internal shell. The belemnoid shell was divided into three principal parts —the rostrum, the fragmocone, and the proostracum.

The rostrum, solid calcite and therefore more commonly preserved, was usually cigar-shaped; in some species, however, it was flattened. There were slender types as well as chunky ones. The apex ended in a sharp point, was rounded, or had a protuberance called a mucro. Ornamentation on the rostrum included granulations and grooves; these are used in classification because they are believed to be traces of muscle insertions that were connected with the animal's body.

The upper portion of the rostrum had a conical depression into which the fragmocone fitted. This most important part of the shell is rarely found in the fossil state because of its fragility. Basically, it consisted of a cone divided by circular walls, which were traversed by a siphon (possibly a siphuncle) located in a ventral position.

Because of the presence of the walls and the siphon, the fragmocone corresponded to the similar part of the shell on the ammonites and nautiluses, and must have

served the same function of enabling the animal to move up and down in the water. In the best-preserved examples, the walls leave characteristic lines of insertion, similar to the suture lines on the ammonites.

The cone extended dorsally into a very delicate elongate structure, the proostracum. This, too, is rarely preserved, for not only was it extremely fragile, but it was impregnated with aragonite, a mineral much more soluble than calcite.

The belemnoids lived on the surface of the sea or along the coasts. Because of their wide geographical distribution, their larvae are believed to have been planktonic in their habits, and the various forms of the shell can be explained as adaptations to different ways of life. Predatory creatures, the belemnoids were, in turn, easy prey for the huge sharks that lived at that time.

Three Belemnite fossil shells belong to three genera of the subclass Dibranchia:
A. Belemnites, *from the Lower Jurassic*
B. Aulacoceras, *from the Triassic period*
C. Duvalia, *from the Lower Cretaceous*

A shell of Nautilus pompilius (opposite page) is cut in half to show the compartmentalization. The adjacent drawing shows the parts of a typical nautilus:

1. tentacles
2. mantle
3. walls
4. chamber
5. siphuncle
6. gonad
7. digestive tube
8. gills
9. oral bulb (mouth)
10. funnel

Nautiluses—Tetrabranchia

The subclass Tetrabranchia is represented by a single genus, *Nautilus*, of the family Nautilidae and the order Nautiloidea. The genus includes only five species surviving from the thousands existing in the geological past. The best known is the chambered, or pearly, nautilus, *Nautilus pompilius*.

All the tetrabranchs, living and extinct, share one common characteristic—an external shell. And of the cephalopods still living, they are the only animals to have that structure. They are unique in another respect, too. Many mollusks enlarge their shells as they grow larger, moving into the larger quarters and often sealing off the abandoned areas. But only in the nautilus are abandoned chambers filled with a gas that helps to make the heavy shell more buoyant.

The tropical seas of the South Pacific and the Indian Ocean are the only areas inhabited by pearly nautiluses. Their normal size ranges from 4 to 6 inches, but specimens up to 10 inches in diameter are known.

Shells. Almost invariably the shell is brown striped and has a pearly luster when cleaned. The inside of the shell is mother-of-pearl and colored in shades ranging from pink to aquamarine.

Ordinarily, when nautiluses are found on the surface they are dead or dying, for these creatures live on the bottom. Floating shells are common, however, because of the gas trapped in the inner chambers, which gives the shell a buoyancy of its own after the animal has been removed.

As with the fossil species, the gas-filled chambers of the nautilus enable the shell to function as a hydrostatic organ. The animal can move vertically in the water simply by emerging from the living chamber or going back in. Out, it diminishes its specific gravity by increasing its volume; in, it reverses the process.

Anatomy. When seen in the shallows with its body expanded, the nautilus bears no resemblance to other cephalopods. Instead of 8 or 10 arms, it has about 90 slender tentacles arranged in rows around its mouth and eyes. With these tentacles spread out, waiting for prey, it looks like a large sea anemone attached to a shell. And like the sea anemone, the nautilus can instantly withdraw its tentacles at the first sign of danger, for each fits into a little sheath.

The nautilus has partially calcified jaws that vaguely resemble a parrot's beak. Perhaps the strangest feature is its eyes, which are simple and thought to act on the same principle as a pinhole camera. They are like miniature bowls with a thin skin stretched across the opening. In the center is a tiny opening, and water filling the cavity acts as a lens. No other creature is known to have eyes of this type.

Below the eyes are the olfactory organs, which are located in cavities connected to

The shell of a belemnite is the only part of the animal that has been preserved by fossilization. The shell, which was internal, was divided into three parts:

1. proostracum
2. phragmocone
3. rostrum

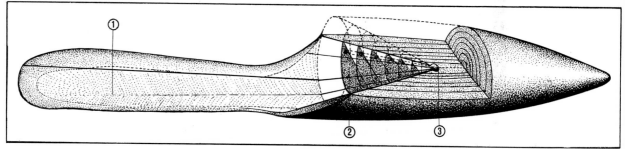

the nervous system. The short tentacles in the vicinity of the eyes may also serve this purpose. Outside the hard brain cartilage is a pair of statocysts, the organs that enable the nautilus to maintain its equilibrium. The nervous system is the simplest among the cephalopods.

The single gonad is lodged in the rear of the body cavity. Only the right genital duct maintains its function; in the male it is divided into sections, one of which is the pouch of the spermatophore. The female has a single nidamental gland, which produces material for covering the eggs. After laying her eggs, she attaches them to the sea floor.

Squids, Octopuses, and Cuttlefish—Dibranchia

Squids and octopuses are eaten in many parts of the world. In Spain they are sometimes baked in their own ink. They are also used in Italian cooking in spaghetti sauces, and in various Chinese dishes. The subclass Dibranchia includes the octopuses, squids, cuttlefish, and argonauts. All of these animals have two gills and either an internal shell or no shell.

Anatomy. The octopuses have eight arms; the squids and cuttlefish have ten. The arms

A close-up view of the tentacles of a Nautilus *protruding from the shell. There are about 94 of these food-grasping organs in the female and about 60 in the male. Most of them are arranged in rings around the mouth, the others around the eyes. When all its tentacles, which can be retracted, are extended, the* Nautilus *looks like a sea anemone attached to a shell.*

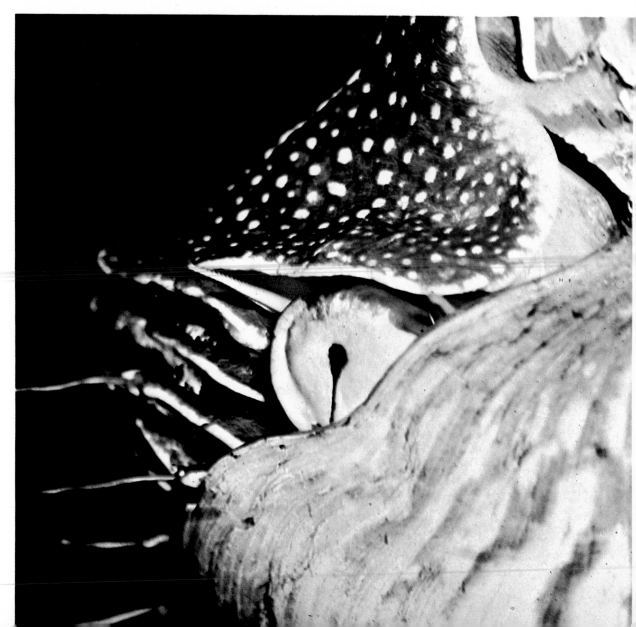

growths located on the head behind the eyes.

The nervous system of these active animals is quite highly developed. A large brain, encircling the esophagus, lies between the eyes. It is unusual in that it consists of several pairs of ganglia fused together. In less well-developed systems, the nerve centers are diffused, and are found in various parts of the body.

These cephalopods have two gills and a closed circulatory system in which the blood flows within vessels, passing from the arteries to the veins through capillaries. It distributes oxygen rapidly through the tissues. The tissues are permeated with networks of capillaries, and gaseous exchanges take place rapidly through their thin walls. Separate pumping mechanisms move blood through the gills and to the tissues. Deoxygenated blood returning from the tissues enters two gill, or branchial, hearts, one for each gill. These help to move blood through the gills at a higher pressure. Freshly oxygenated blood from the gills enters the systemic heart, which pumps it out again to the tissues.

The round mouth, located within the circle of arms, is surrounded by a lip. Inside the lip are two powerful horny jaws, which bite vertically with great force, tearing at food held in the grasp of the arms. The radula, when present, is used to draw food into the mouth.

As food passes through the esophagus to the stomach, various glands pour out secretions to aid in digestion. In many species the stomach is a muscular grinding organ similar to a bird's gizzard. Digestion is completed in the intestine, aided by other secretions. Waste products are passed to the anus, which opens into the mantle cavity, and are discharged through the funnel.

Ink Secretion. In the mantle cavity, just behind the funnel, most cephalopods have a gland for secreting ink. This is a thick, dark-

Nautilus macromphalus of New Caledonia (left) belongs to the only surviving genus of the hundreds that once made up the Tetrabranchia. These animals usually stay on the ocean bottoms. When they travel to upper waters, gases inside their shell chambers help to equalize water pressure and add to their bouyancy in the water.

are equipped with suckers or hooks—some species have both. The ten arms of the Decapoda normally have telescoping suckers reinforced by a horny ring or by hooks. Each of the eight arms of the Octopoda has a row or more of nontelescoping suckers, without horny rings, running along the entire length.

In most of these animals the muscles are well developed. But in some deep-water species, such as *Chunioteuthis mollis,* the body has a gelatinous consistency similar to that of a jellyfish. The muscles are inserted into the cephalic capsule, which is a mass of protective cartilage in the head functioning somewhat like the skull in a vertebrate. It is attached to the surface of the internal shell, when one exists.

The eyes, as we mentioned previously, are remarkably similar to those of man and the other vertebrates, although not all the parts find a parallel. In some species the eyes are fixed; in others, they protrude or are telescopic. The latter condition is true mainly of the open-sea species, especially in the early stages of their development.

Included in the head cartilage are a pair of stabilizers, the statocysts. The olfactory organs are small cavities, warts, or other brown liquid, so strong that a few drops can color and cloud a large amount of water. The ink cloud is used in defense to confuse an attacker.

Octopuses, which are sedentary creatures, will usually put out the ink screen while at rest, and then attempt to escape under its cover. They may, however, discharge it steadily while swimming. They can do this because the gland secretes ink constantly and sends it into a reservoir that the animal can draw upon at will. The coloring agents in the ink are copper and iron, extracted from the cephalopod's blood.

Color Change. Cephalopods of this group have the ability to change color. The changes in color result from the expansion and contraction of *chromatophores,* or pigment cells, located on the animal's body. These cells often contain different pigments, and certain individuals are quite capable of turning all colors of the rainbow. Sometimes the colors are sharply defined; sometimes they blend in with each other harmoniously, the patterns shifting and changing. The octopuses have developed this capacity to the highest degree, and can rapidly change their color to match their background.

Most species change color when frightened, and many undergo color changes as part of their courtship and mating behavior.

In addition, some species are luminescent. The power to produce light, some scientists believe, is more highly developed in certain squids than in any other animal. The fact that most luminescent cephalopods are inhabitants of the deep has limited opportunities to observe the phenomenon fully, however. The light-producing organs can occur almost anywhere on the body of the animal, but are most often found on the arms, on the mantle sac, in the eye, and in the mantle cavity. Often these organs are internal, and the luminescence is visible only because of the transparency of the body tissues of the live animal. In some species luminescence is due to the presence of luminescent bacteria, and in some even the ink is luminescent.

Squids. The squids, members of the order Decapoda, have 10 appendages—8 arms and 2 longer tentacles. In some species the arms are all the same length, in some they are unequal in length, and in others, adjacent arms are partly joined by a web between them. Squids are found in all seas and at various depths, ranging down to 5,000 feet or more. The deep-sea forms may have soft bodies, rather like jellyfish.

The shell of the squid, the pen, varies in shape from broad and flat to slender and lancelike. In the smallest species it is only a fraction of an inch in length, while in the giant squid it is several feet long.

There are five families of squids, including the 60-foot giant squids, and the sea arrows, or flying squids, which can leap 15 feet out of the water. Of the 80 squid species that have been recorded in the Western Hemisphere, more than 70 are found in the waters off North America.

Squids of the family Onychoteuthidae are of medium and large size and are particularly agile. Their arms are very long; two rows of hooks and two rows of suckers are present on each arm.

Onychoteuthis banksi is found in all seas. It is generally brownish in color with blue around the eyes. It is about 6 inches long.

Streamlined for speed, the Ommastrephidae include the sea arrows, or flying squid, as well as the giant squid. Long, slender animals with cylindrical bodies, their terminal fins meet in a point, giving them the appearance of an arrow-head. They are often seen in swarms, swimming swiftly with fins foremost and arms trailing behind. Their great speed enables members of the Ommastrephidae to build up enough momentum to leap far out of the water.

These swift killers are like efficient machines as they swoop down on a school of mackerel or herring. They strike right and left, grasping fish with their sucker-clad arms and holding them as they bite quickly with their sharp beaks. They devour their prey with great haste, and continue killing even after they have eaten their fill.

The sea arrows are members of the genus *Ommastrephes. O. illecebrosus* is commonly found along the east coast of North America from the Gulf of Mexico northward. It is about 1 foot in length, and is commonly shaded with blue and red and sometimes spotted.

For sheer size, no invertebrate can match *Architeuthis princeps,* the giant squid. The shell, or pen, of this squid may be 4 feet long. The giant squid's reputation in literature is probably more than a little exaggerated. It is, nonetheless, a fearsome animal, and commonly grows to 50 or 60 feet in length. Huge sperm whales caught by whalers often show large circular scars on their tough hides left by the suckers of a giant squid during a battle. In these battles, the whale invariably wins.

Squid of the family Loliginidae have long, cylindrical bodies that taper to a point. An internal horny shell, the pen, is as long as the mantle.

In the common American squid, *Loligo pealei,* the paired triangular fins are united at the end and extend more than halfway up the animal's body. A double row of suckers runs along each of the eight fixed arms, and the bulbous ends of the tentacles, called clubs, have four or more rows of suckers. The third pair of arms is the longest; the left arm of the fourth, or lowest, pair modifies into a hectocotylus during breeding periods. The suckers at its tip become swollen with sperm-carrying capsules called spermatophores. These are transferred to a horseshoe-shaped receptacle located on the membrane inside the female's mouth cavity, where they are held until her eggs are ready for fertilization.

The same pair of squids may mate several times in a few hours, and an especially

The diagram (below right) shows a dissection of a female cuttlefish with the wall of the visceral sac removed. The labeled parts are:
  1. excretory orifice
  2. gills
  3. nidamental gland
  4. ink pouch with gonad behind it
  5. genital orifice
  6. anus

The diagram (below left) includes the following labeled parts:
  1. funnel
  2. esophagus
  3. liver
  4. intestine
  5. gills
  6. nephridium
  7, 8. branchial heart with appendage
  9. gonad
  10. crop
  11. mouth

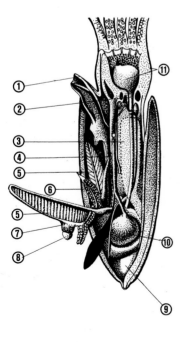

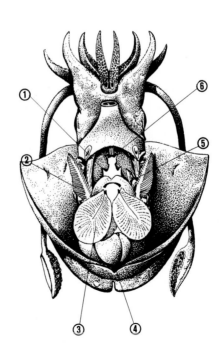

vigorous male may seize the female so ardently that he kills her.

After spawning, many smaller species of squid die. Those that live pay no attention to their eggs. The jellylike case apparently is distasteful to all sea creatures except the iron-stomached starfish *Patiria miniata,* and even this eater-of-anything takes about three full days to digest a string of squid's eggs.

Loligo opalescens is a squid found along the coast of California. It is about 2 feet long and is fished commercially.

The name of the family Sepiolidae suggests correctly a resemblance to the cuttlefish (family Sepiidae). These squids are, however, considerably smaller, usually attaining a length of only a few inches at most. In this family, the body is short and shaped rather like a thimble, although sometimes it is globular. The fins are rounded and located near the middle of the body. The arms generally have numerous rows of suckers, while the tentacles and their clubs have only two. The male's first left arm serves as the hectocotylus. The well-developed eyes possess both lens and cornea.

Rossia hyatti ranges from Newfoundland to Massachusetts in depths of from 10 to 200 fathoms. It has a pinkish color, spotted with purplish brown, with the front edge of the mantle and the insides of the arms a paler color. The large, round head and the top of the body are covered with whitish, conical growths. The eyes are large, with prominent lower lids. The arms are short and joined near their bases by a web.

R. sublevis is common along the northeast coast of North America at depths of from 40 to about 150 fathoms. It is about 2 inches long, and is pink and brownish with spots. *R. pacifica* is found along the Pacific coast from Alaska to southern California. It is about 3½ inches in length.

The butterfly squid, *Stoloteuthis leucoptera,* is a rather rare animal found at depths of 100 fathoms off the coast of north-

ern New England. It is a little over an inch long, with very large, long, transparent fins. Its dorsal surface is covered with bright rust-colored spots, while the undersides are brown and blue.

The peacock squid, *Loligopsis pavo,* is a member of the family Cranchiidae. It is about 3 feet long and is found from New England to the Arctic. It is red with spots.

Spirula. Spirula spirula, the only member of the family Spirulidae, is one of the least familiar of the cephalopods. Sometimes called a cuttlefish, it is found in nearly all tropical and subtropical seas. Although they are rarely caught, their shells wash ashore on all the continents, sometimes by the thousands.

Seldom exceeding ½ inch in diameter, the tiny shells consist of two or three loose coils. This descendent of the fossil *Belemnites* of the Mesozoic era has eight short fixed arms, equal in size and fitted with numerous small suckers, and two retractile tentacles. The body, which is about 3 inches long including tentacles, is cylindrical, with a rounded end. It is usually brown or red with brown spots.

This animal has long been a problem to science. Systematists now agree that it is related to the cuttlefish, and many zoologists now rebut the traditional belief that the shell is partly internal and partly external. Those who have been able to observe the animal alive insist that the shell is completely enclosed by the mantle. They point out that, when the creature is preserved, the mantle is often frayed, allowing the shell to protrude and mistaken conclusions to be drawn.

Cuttlefish. The cuttlefish are members of the family Sepiidae. Their calcareous shell, the cuttlebone, includes a rostrum and a modified fragmocone with air chambers, but no siphuncle.

Cuttlefish are not found in the waters around North America. They live in the

Atlantic, but along the European coast. They are most common in the Mediterranean, the western Pacific, and the Indian Ocean, generally in shallow coastal waters. There are about 80 species, varying in size from *Hemisepius typicus*, 3 inches long with tentacles fully extended, to *Sepia latimanus*, with a 2-foot mantle and an overall length of 5 feet.

The body of the cuttlefish is flattened and oval. The margins of the mantle form two long, narrow fins. The eight arms are short, with stalked, horny-rimmed suckers in four rows. Two long tentacles, retracted into pockets below the eyes, can shoot out to capture such prey as fishes and crustaceans. This animal's internal shell (the cuttlebone of canary cages) is shaped like a shield and

runs almost the entire length of the mantle. Made of calcareous material secreted by the mantle, it contains a series of air chambers but no siphuncle. In proportion to body size, it is the largest internal shell of the cephalopods. Its light, chambered structure strengthens the cuttlefish's body and at the same time gives it added buoyancy.

The cuttlefish can control its specific gravity by means of changing the proportions of gas and liquid contained in the internal shell, or cuttlebone. When the cuttlefish pumps liquid out of the cuttlebone it thus makes room for more gas, which is largely nitrogen. This in turn means that the cuttlefish is less dense. It increases its density by the reverse process—by pumping

The squid Illex illecebrosus *feeds on fishes, crustaceans, and other mollusks. This picture clearly shows the prominent eyes, the numerous ringed suckers on the arms, the elongated fins, and the chromatophores, or pigment cells, located on the animal's body.*

more liquid into the cuttlebone.

Although cuttlefish swim more slowly than octopuses, they tend to be more active. They swim by undulating their narrow marginal fins. But the funnel on the underside of the cuttlefish's body is crucial when speed is necessary. By expelling a strong stream of water the animal can drive itself speedily in the opposite direction. Of course, the funnel can be turned in any direction, enabling the cuttlefish to "jet propel" itself to any point. The funnel also enables the animal to remain in one place. Appearing quite motionless, the cuttlefish nonetheless

is aiming its funnel in one direction and then another, emitting small puffs. This activity is accompanied by fin motion, to keep the animal more-or-less stationary. The funnel is also the channel for ejecting the protective ink.

Cuttlefish are able to change their colors more rapidly and in a greater variety of shades than other mollusks—perhaps even more so than any other color-changing animal. Basically gray, a cuttlefish has cromatophores, or pigment-bearing cells, enabling it to become mostly yellow, orange, red, brown, or black, or a combination of these

hues. Cuttlefish change color to accord with their environment of the moment, apparently receiving the stimulus for this transformation through the eyes. Cuttlefish travel in schools, and all of them in a given group change color together.

The fourth left arm of the male cuttlefish is transformed into a hectocotylus for breeding. Females lay black eggs, as large as hazelnuts, in clusters. Washed up on the beach, a cluster of eggs looks like a bunch of grapes—hence the name sea grapes.

The best-known species is the common cuttlefish, *Sepia officinalis*, which has a maximum length of about 15 inches. Since the tentacles can extend about 20 inches, its overall length is about 3 feet. It is common in the Mediterranean and is used for food in some European countries. It is brown with white stripes and spots, and the fins are purple.

Sepia officinalis was described in detailed terms first by the great 4th-century B.C. Greek philosopher and scientist, Aristotle. But for centuries before Aristotle, cuttlefish were caught in the Mediterranean—even as they are to this day. And to this day fishermen continue to exploit the cuttlefishes' mating urges to snare them. One technique involves placing branches just offshore for the females to lay their grapelike eggs on. Males pursue the spawning females to shore. After the eggs are laid, the fishermen gather up as many cuttlefish, by whatever means, as they can.

A rather more insidious, although still traditional, method of catching cuttlefish involves towing a female on a line behind a boat at a depth of a few feet. Attracting males after her, she continues on the tow. The fishermen net the males—and sometimes the females if they cannot be separated. But the female is tossed back—always on the line—to entrap more males, however involuntarily.

Octopuses. Of all the cephalopods, the octopuses are the best known. They are also among the most misunderstood, for they are not at all as ferocious as fables and fancies would have us believe. As a matter of fact, they are basically placid, sedentary creatures who would rather run than fight. A relatively unknown member of the order Octopoda is the argonaut, a cephalopod with a thin, spiral shell.

There are between 150 and 200 species of octopuses living in almost all the seas from pole to pole. All the more common spe-

one pair of arms two or three times the size of the others. Suckers are arranged in one or two rows down the arm, and are not stalked or equipped with horny rings. Some of the deep-sea species have webs reaching almost to the tips of the arms.

Octopuses usually have a large head, with only a slightly narrowed neck at its junction with the body. Only a few species have fins. There is no shell. The eyes are prominent; the head is usually enlarged around them and concave in between. In size these animals vary from the 2-inch *Octopus arbor-*

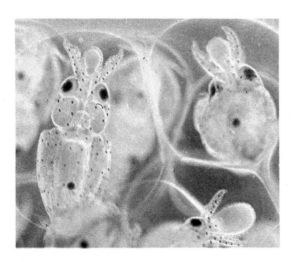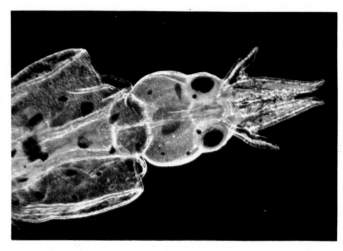

Embryos of the squid Alloteuthis subulata *(this page and opposite page bottom), of the east Atlantic Ocean, are shown in advanced stages of development.*

cies live in shallow water. A number of others, however, live in deep seas—exactly how far down no one knows. Trawls have brought up octopuses from as deep as four miles, but there is no proof that the creatures entered the trawl at that depth. One specimen, however, was taken at more than 2,400 fathoms with bottom-dwelling animals in its stomach. And an octopus egg was found in the stomach of a fish trawled from 3,600 fathoms.

Octopuses have eight arms. These spring from the head, which is bulbous and pear-shaped, and are united at the base by a membranous web. In most cases the arms are of equal length, but there are species with

escens to the large *Octopus hongkongensis* of the Pacific. One of the latter, taken in Alaskan waters, had arms that were 16 feet long. These arms grew extremely slender toward the tips. The body was comparatively slight, measuring only 18 inches.

The common octopus of Europe, *Octopus vulgaris*, was known as Polypus in ancient times and was accurately described by Aristotle. It lives along rocky shores at moderate depths, making its home in a cave where it lurks waiting to rush out and seize any bivalve or fish that strays too close. Its cephalopodian ability to harmonize in color with its surroundings serves it well—its body can be mistaken for a rock.

Like all the dibranchs, octopuses display remarkable intelligence in their hunting habits. They will creep along in the wake of a scuttling crab, using their arms much as a vertebrate uses its legs. Or they swim along above, waiting for an opportunity to swoop down on the unsuspecting prey. Sometimes an octopus will catch several victims in rapid succession, holding them helpless with its suckers while it pursues others. Once the captives disappear under the cephalopod's mantle, life is over in seconds. The powerful beak of the octopus crunches off claws, and the suckered arms wrench carapaces or valves apart with ease.

In addition to the beak, many octopuses also use poison to finish off their victims. The venom is secreted by the posterior salivary glands. Just how it is injected is not known; some zoologists believe it is absorbed through the gills of the prey. The poison is toxic and fast acting; it paralyzes and then kills crabs in as little as 45 seconds.

Observations have led investigators of octopus behavior to the conclusion that these cephalopods generally attack only moving objects. Octopuses are attracted by the movements of their small prey. Despite the numerous reports through the years of octopuses grabbing and holding people, it is not at all certain how frequently this has actually happened. Probably it has occurred at times in the warmer seas of the world, but these instances are believed to be rare. Bcause it is thought that the octopus does not deliberately attack a person but is only investigating a moving entity, a person in an octopus' clutches is advised to remain motionless— perhaps a difficult thing to do in the circumstances. Presumably, if the person keeps quite still, the octopus will investigate the person by feel for a short period and then release him.

This reassuring advice, however, must certainly be disregarded when it concerns species of the genus *Hapalochlaena*—and perhaps of other genera. The popular name for these octopuses, which are usually about 8 inches in length from the tip of one arm across the body to the tip of the opposite arm, is blue-ringed octopus. They are common around Australia and, indeed, throughout the south and southeast Pacific.

The blue-ringed octopus at rest is rather variable in color, but basically brownish with darker bands over the body and arms. These bands are circled by light blue lines. The coloration becomes darker when the animal is bothered.

An adult Sepiola rondeleti *(directly below), is similar in form to a cuttlefish. These animals are much smaller, however, reaching a maximum length of only a few inches. Like their larger relatives, they have the characteristic ink sac from which they can expel a cloud of dark liquid to confuse their enemies.*

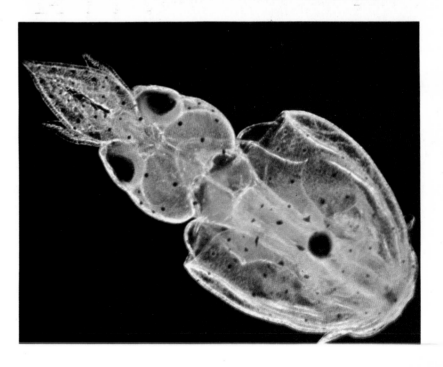

In recent years blue-ringed octopuses caused several deaths and more near-deaths on Australian coasts. Attracted by the blue rings and often brilliant colors of the animal, people picked it up in the surf. Within minutes—often without the victim's feeling the bite—the octopus' poison is at work. The victim feels weakness, numbness, and then dies of respiratory failure.

In male octopuses, the third arm on the right side is hectocotylized—specialized for the storage and deposition of sperm. The male caresses the female with the tip of that arm and then inserts it into her mantle cavity beside the funnel. The two animals may remain this way for hours, the female quiet except for spasmodic movements, the male moving its arms only slightly as the sperm-carrying capsules move down a longitudinal groove.

Octopus bimaculatus varies in color from white to almost black, and is about 4 inches in length. It is found along the Pacific coast of North America from southern California to Lower California. It can be identified by a pair of blue spots halfway between the eyes and the third pair of arms.

Octopus briareus, a familiar species in the waters off Florida, provides a good ex-

ample of the color-changing capacities of the cephalopods. It can be brown one minute and a greenish-blue the next, depending on the situation. Next it may become reddish, or even an almost pure white. Most impressive, perhaps, is the ability of *O. briareus* to display different colors on opposite sides of its body.

This octopus species is among those that have been much observed and studied in laboratories. A female *O. briareus* in a Florida aquarium demonstrated the learning ability of octopuses, which with squids possess the most complicated brains of any invertebrates. This specimen was actually trained to open a bottle. The trainer began by putting a shrimp in a specially designed glass jar, the hole of which was unstopped. After the octopus learned to cope with the clear glass, finding the hole to recover the shrimp bait, a cork was balanced over the hole. Patiently, the trainer taught the octopus to remove the inserted cork, even when it had been pressed in tight. The animal's record at opening the bottle to retrieve the shrimp was eventually established at ten minutes.

Octopus bairdi is about 3½ inches long and whitish marked with brown. It is found in moderately deep waters along the northeast coast of North America and the northern coasts of Europe.

This octopus (below) was photographed inside an aquarium. Its bulbous body pouch and the webbing at the base of its arms are clearly visible. An octopus feeds mainly on crustaceans, such as crabs and lobsters, however, it will also eat fish and other mollusks. Its arm suckers are important in catching and holding the prey.

Argonauts. The argonauts, or paper nautiluses, belong to the genus *Argonauta* of the family Argonautidae. People observing them centuries ago, sailing over the water behind a paper-thin shell that looked like a sail, gave them the name *nautilus,* which means "little sailor." The writers of ancient Greece and Rome called them *Argonauta* after the Argonauts of myth who sailed with Jason for the Golden Fleece.

Even though they had been seen at close hand for hundreds of years, these creatures remained an enigma until the last century. The ancients had noticed that the animal was not connected by tissue to its shell. Thus

Two octopuses (left and below) lie among the rocks, watching for prey. Their bodies and even their huge eyes blend into the background. When it spots a suitable prey, an octopus may creep along behind it or swim above it, waiting for the chance to pounce. If it is hungry enough, an octopus will eat members of its own species.

they assumed that, like the hermit crab, the argonaut appropriated some other animal's shell—probably that of an unknown large snail—as its own. This was a commonly accepted belief until 1839, when Mme. Jeannette Power announced the results of observations she had made over a lengthy period of time at a marine aquarium in Italy.

Madame Power watched argonaut eggs hatch into tiny shell-less creatures. Then, 10 or 12 days later, she saw certain individuals begin to form shells by secretions from glands on two arms held close together. The shell, keeled in the center and delicately

sculptured with parallel ridges as new sections were added, grew with the animal. The argonaut rested in the mouth of the shell, which the two weblike arms clasped tightly. When the animal was mature, it laid its eggs in the shell, thus proving that it was not a proper shell at all, but an egg cradle.

While Mme. Power was making these observations, another mystery was nearing solution. All the argonauts seen so far had been females. How were the female's eggs fertilized? Where was the male? Earlier in the century, scientists had discovered in the mantle of female argonauts small bodies that looked like parasitic worms. Because these worms resembled the arm of a cephalopod, they were given the name *hectocotylus,* meaning "arm of a hundred suckers," and a new genus of worms was born.

Later, however, some zoologists began to doubt the validity of this theory. Albert Kolliker, a Swiss, made a detailed study of the alleged worm and pointed out that almost everything about it related directly to the cephalopods, including sperm cells carried in a small cavity. Kolliker, on the brink of truth, made a wrong turn. He announced that the hectocytylus was really the male argonaut, which bodily entered the female to fertilize the eggs.

Finally, in 1853, the German zoologist Heinrich Muller solved the problem. As he studied some very small argonauts that had no shell he discovered, coiled in a sack hidden among the arms, a hectocotylus. These tiny shell-less argonauts, about ½ inch long, were the long-sought males whose arms developed into hectocotyluses.

Later observations showed how the hectocotylus works. A specialized part of an arm, it breaks away from the arm on which it grew and swims under its own power—looking much like a worm, as a matter of fact—until it reaches a female and fixes itself in her mantle cavity with its suckers! The only other cephalopods known to have detachable and autonomous hectocotyli are the octopuses of the genera *Ocythoe* and *Tremoctopus.*

Vampire Squids. The vampire sqiuds of the order Vampyromorpha are small octopus-like animals that are found in deep water. They have eight arms with webbing between them and two small tentacles. The principal genus of the group is *Vampyroteuthis.*

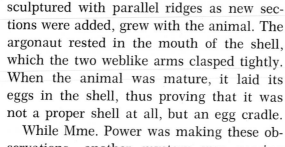

The octopus Eledone cirrosa (right) *is relatively small. It lives in the western Mediterranean and the Adriatic. This photo shows its streamlined shape as it swims past an underwater grotto.*

DATE DUE

OCT 23		
APR 30		
MAY 15		
DEC 15		
NOV. 15		
MAY 11		
OCT. 14		
NOV. 5		
MAR. 10		
JAN. 21		
OCT 12		

VOL. 17

ILLUS. ENCY. OF THE ANIMAL
KINGDOM

MOLLUSKS

DATE DUE	BORROWER'S NAME	ROOM NUMBER

VOL. 17

ILLUS. ENCY OF THE ANIMAL KINGDOM

MOLLUSKS